a time to speak

to everything there is a season,
and a time to every purpose under the heaven: . . .
a time to keep silence, and a time to speak.

a time to speak

or
how to prepare
and present a speech

wil a. linkugel
university of kansas

david m. berg
university of kansas

wadsworth publishing company, inc.
belmont, california

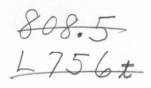
chapter opening illustrations by mona berg

© 1970 by wadsworth publishing company, inc., belmont, california 94002. all rights reserved. no part of this book may be reproduced, stored in a retrieval system, or transcribed, in any form or by any means, electronic, mechanical, photocopying, recording, or otherwise, without the prior written permission of the publisher.

l. c. cat. card no.: 71–98339
printed in the united states of america

1 2 3 4 5 6 7 8 9 10—74 73 72 71 70

Another semester is over. Facing his class for the last time, the professor of public speaking is spending the final period discussing the merits and demerits of the course with his students. Not being of the silent generation, the young scholars speak freely. The discussion has been going on for some time when finally the professor asks: "And what did you think of the textbook? John, did it serve your needs?"

John   I don't know. I didn't read it.

Professor   Well! No wonder you only got a "C" on the midterm. How about the rest of you? What did you think of the book?

Rest of the students (almost in unison)   It was awful.

Professor   But I chose the book that has the most substance.

Students   But you mistake words for substance. The book has far too many pages that are neither practical, profound, or interesting. One has to wade through reams of pages to uncover relatively few and simple concepts essential to the actual preparation and delivery of a speech.

Professor   Well, if you are so sure you know what you want perhaps you can give me a set of criteria you think I should use in selecting a textbook for next year.

Students   Gladly. One: It should be totally practical. Two: It should be short. Three: It should be interesting. Our old book covers far too many things that don't really matter anyway. If you feel that you must have us read more for the course to be respectable, give us thought-stimulating materials to read and study or, for that matter, some good speeches for analysis and study would be far more meaningful.

Professor   But it is very hard to make theoretical concepts interesting.

Students   But even you yourself say, "There are no dull subjects; just dull speakers." A good rhetorician should thus be able to make even rhetoric interesting!

Combined, we have twenty-five years of teaching experience. We have enacted the above dialogue, or something like it, many times. We have written this book with that dialogue in mind. Our aim is to present and illustrate established major concepts of public speaking in as brief and interesting a way as possible, leaving out all that's extraneous, striving to be ever practical. Our intended audience is the inexperienced speaker, be he a student in a beginning speech course or an adult who finds it is time to speak in public.

The approach of this book is not intended to minimize the value of those works that deal with speechmaking from an historical and theoretical perspective. We feel simply that, while such material is necessary for a comprehensive treatment of speech communication generally, it is not essential to the development of basic skill in preparing and presenting speeches. We think that our teaching will be much better received by students in the basic speech course if we focus on a few concepts, make them truly meaningful, and present them in an interesting way.

To increase the chances of using supplementary materials with it, this book is produced in a paperback edition. We suggest two kinds: (1) a collection of speeches for critical study and analysis—such as *Contemporary American Speeches;** and (2) a book of readings, rich in additional insights into the speech process, for class discussion. The book may thus be

---

* Wil A. Linkugel, R. R. Allen, and Richard L. Johannesen, *Contemporary American Speeches*, 2nd ed. (Belmont, Calif.: Wadsworth Publishing Company, Inc., 1969).

used singly for a short course, or it may be used in concert with one or both of the other two kinds of materials cited. We feel that the teacher of public speaking should have his students read a significant amount, but that the assigned readings should be more provocative than the average chapter of a textbook on fundamentals of speech.

We wish to acknowledge Brad Lashbrook, Tim Kelley, Cheri Tibbetts, Donna Lasseter, and Ernie Link, all students, who gave us permission to quote from their speeches. We are also indebted to Charles E. Ledbetter of Thornton Junior College and Robert J. Minton of the College of Marin for their thoughtful and encouraging reviews of the manuscript.

w.a.l.
d.m.b.

contents

contents

a time to speak

1

the speaker as "number one"

Playboy magazine not long ago published a cartoon that appeared to have been inspired by artist James Whistler's famous painting of his mother. Ensconced in her favorite chair was the characteristic little old lady—kindly expression, hair in a bun, rimless glasses, knitting in her lap—with her faithful cat curled up at her feet. On the wall above her head hung an old-fashioned needlework sampler with its simple hand-stitched motto. It read: *"Watch Out For Number One."*

This message, however inconsistent with our image of little old ladies, provides an appropriate opening to a book written for the beginning public speaker. We don't mean to imply by this, of course, that such people are intrinsically more egotistical or self-centered than any other group. It is clear, however, that the public speaking situation is highly relevant to a number of basic human needs, particularly as these are felt by the speaker himself. As such, it's understandable that those who enter this situation in the role of speaker are, in almost all cases, primarily concerned with the satisfaction of their own needs.

For this reason we approach the subject of public speaking from what may be referred to as a *speaker-oriented* point of view. For those who have given little thought to the nature of communication, it may come as something of a surprise that there can be any other approach to the subject. The study of public speaking, however, may be profitably initiated from the viewpoint of any of its major, interrelated components—audience, message, situation, as well as speaker. Within the following pages, all these factors will, of course, be considered—but always as they relate to the needs and goals of you, the speaker.

our need to express and communicate

"I celebrate myself, and sing myself," wrote poet Walt Whitman, and so does each of us. For self-expression is a basic human need, which no man can ignore if he is to realize his full potential. From the first cry at birth, all of us have of necessity discovered means of expressing ourselves, and through this expression we have contributed to our growth and development as distinctive human beings.

But just as the need for expression is basic to human existence, so is our need to communicate with others. French philosopher Georges Gusdorf has observed: "On the one hand, we have the expressive function of language: I speak in order to make myself understood, in order to emerge into reality, in order to add myself to nature. On the other hand, we have the communicative function: I speak in order to reach out to others."[1] The importance of this reaching out is dramatically illustrated in the following story told by a clergyman:

> I was in my church office late one mid-week evening preparing for the next Sunday's service. Without warning, the outside door burst open and I found myself facing a disheveled, ashen-faced man waving a gun. Without a word, he motioned me to my chair, where I sat in silence as he paced the room. Several times it looked as though he would speak, but it must have been five or ten minutes before any words came out. At first he talked slowly—haltingly—telling of a grocery store robbery earlier in the evening, then of a childhood without love, a business failure, an unsuccessful mar-

[1] Georges Gusdorf, *Speaking*, trans. Paul T. Brockelman (Evanston, Ill.: Northwestern University Press, 1965), p. 50.

riage. As I listened he came closer, finally sitting in the chair across the desk from me. Then, as he finished his story, he placed the gun on the desk, pushed it toward me, and asked that I call the police.

Later, when they were taking him away, he thanked me for talking with him. It was only then that I realized I had never really said anything at all.

The need felt most strongly by this tragic figure—to be in contact, to communicate, with another human being—is a need shared by millions in today's world. It is a pathetic fact that at this time in many of our nation's cities there are those who hire themselves out, not as advisers, but only as someone to talk with.

Communication is integrally related not only to this universal compulsion to reach out to other human beings during time of stress, but also to our powers of creativity. Such powers wither and die in those unable to maintain contacts outside themselves. Richard Wagner, the great German composer, attests to this loss in a letter to a friend written during one of the many unhappy periods of his life:

> Deprived of all stimulation from the tangible world, continually reduced to feeding on myself, I need, in order somewhat to maintain my vital energy, most active and encouraging relations with the external world: after all, whence then would come to me the desire to communicate the depths of my being if I should encounter silence everywhere around me?[2]

In summary, we think it no exaggeration to say that the need to communicate is as basic to human existence as is the need for food. "If we realize," as one study states, "that in order to survive any organism must gain not only the substances necessary for its metabolism but adequate information

[2] Richard Wagner, *Lettres à Hans de Bulow.* From Gusdorf, p. 67.

about the world around it, we see that communication and existence are inseparable concepts."[3]

our need to feel safe

Although the media men employ as vehicles of expression and communication are virtually limitless, no other has the potential of human speech. But further, of the many contexts in which speech may be employed, the public platform is unique as a means of multiplying our contacts and extending our influence. In short, public speaking provides an unexcelled opportunity to each of us for satisfying our need for expression and communication.

the threat of "making a speech"

In spite of the human need for expression and communication, however, when we say to one of our students, "We think you ought to make a speech," we seem to set up a lot of waves, not all of which are waves of pure joy. This is an extraordinary thing about speech students, as well as about people in general, for we have incontrovertible evidence that man is a talking animal; in fact, talking is the thing that defines him best. When you think about it, most people, given a favorable environment, are hard to shut up. The basic human tendency, and it's pretty much universal, is to talk. We observe this in children, we observe it in ourselves, and we may have even gotten into situations where we have been reminded that we talk too much. Such a case was recounted by Bergen Evans, noted author and English professor from Northwestern University, in a speech given at a Macalester College convocation some time ago:

[3] Paul Watzlawick, Janet Beavin, and Don Jackson, *Pragmatics of Human Communication* (New York: W. W. Norton & Co., 1967), p. 258.

I was a house guest at an English country home about twenty years ago. And I was talking in what I thought was rather my better manner when one of the other guests, who had apparently reached the saturation point, interrupted and said, "May I ask you one question?" I walked right into the trap and responded, "Yes, what is it?" He said, "Would you rather that I talked, or would you rather remain ignorant?" I was completely taken off guard, and all I could do was weakly murmur, "Why, sir . . . sir, you speak."

It was two years later before I thought of the answer, and then the man had been dead for over a year. The answer should have been, "Why, sir, let's combine them—you talk!" But that didn't come to me fast enough, and I do hope there is another life that I may hunt that man down somewhere in the Elysian fields. It won't be very effective even then, but it will be some satisfaction.

Clearly, we love our own talk so much that an insulting interruption of it is, as Evans so vividly reminds us, the kind of thing we remember vengefully even twenty years later. But when you take a person who likes to talk, who does a lot of talking, and does it perhaps without much thought about any pressure or any significance except the enjoyment of talk, and you say to him, "I want you to come down to the club next Thursday and make a speech," you do something to his nervous system that is quite frightening. Here's a man who has been talking all of his life who says that he can't make a speech: "Who me? I should make a speech? I don't know how to speak!" This is an absurdity, of course, on the face of it. It is a total irony for a person to say, "I can't make a speech, and if you'll sit down, in the next thirty minutes I'll explain to you in a few thousand well-chosen words why I can't talk." There must be something about this phrase "make a speech" that strikes the nervous system and causes people to freeze up.

Perhaps nowhere has the trauma of the first speech been so painfully detailed as in Eugene Burdick's *The 480*. In the following passage, Burdick describes the initial audience confrontation of his hero, John Thatch:

the speaker as "number one"

In his sophomore year his fraternity ticked him off to run for class vice-president. . . . Thatch memorized a speech. He got to the auditorium, looked down at the five hundred faces, and was struck by a sudden paralyzing fear. Somehow the class, mostly unknown to him, looked ominous. . . . He could not remember a word of the speech. A part of his brain had been seared, the words burned away. Phrases tumbled senselessly through his mind. . . .

He heard his name spoken. He got up and walked woodenly to the podium. Now he waited for it to happen . . . for the synapses to relink, for the magic to work, for his tongue to talk. . . .

Far away, as distant as a surf, he heard a strange sound. It was the sound of laughter. His eyes focused. The five hundred faces were contorted with an expression which must have been laughter. . . .

He stood smiling. And then he was not smiling. . . . His body bent backward, his shoes tilting on their heels. He was falling backward. He came sharply to a dead balance. Then carefully, like a man running from a bull he does not want to provoke into charging, he moved across the stage. The howl deepened and he felt feet stamping in unison.[4]

There isn't much question that Burdick, as a novelist seeking a dramatic effect, placed his hero in an unusually difficult situation for a beginner, as well as caused him to overreact to that situation. It should be of some comfort to us, however, that even after this dismal start John Thatch went on to fame and political success largely as a result of the public speaking ability he was able to develop. Burdick's account of Thatch's first failure, however, does make an important point about public speaking. The point is simply this—the public speaking situation tends to bring two distinctive types of human needs into direct conflict. On the one hand we want to express ourselves, but on the other hand we want to avoid a situation we see as threatening. Our experience as speech teachers has

---

[4] Eugene Burdick, *The 480* (New York: McGraw-Hill, 1964), pp. 96–97.

indicated that the resolution of this apparent dilemma is the principal concern of most of our beginning students.

What happens when human needs come into conflict has been explained most interestingly by psychologist Abraham Maslow in his well-known theory concerning the hierarchy of human needs.[5] The crux of Maslow's explanation is that man is possessed of a sequence of needs, all of which must be realized if he is to achieve his full potential as a human being. The problem is that each succeeding higher need does not become of concern to the individual until the need or needs basic to it have been fulfilled. These "needs," as Maslow identifies them, are, in ascending order: (1) physical, (2) safety, (3) love and esteem, and (4) self-actualization. If all these are successively gratified—that is, if a person can first get enough food, rest, and water; next, reassurance as to freedom from danger to his physical life; then love and esteem from others—then, finally, it will be possible for him to grow toward self-actualization, the point at which most concern for expression and communication will occur. Although we've all heard stories of men who, while starving or suffering other physical deprivation, have produced masterpieces of music, art, or literature, Maslow would argue that these cases are most unusual. His point is that ordinarily when a person is starving he will ignore everything else in his quest for food. When he is in danger of death, he will drop all else in order to save himself. If he is well fed and safe, the affection and love of others will probably become important to him; but it will not be important if he is starving or in danger. Similarly, if he is loved, he may then pursue recognition for achievement. If his affectional needs are in jeopardy, however, the chances are that he will forego these efforts.

[5] Abraham H. Maslow, *Motivation and Personality* (New York: Harper & Row, 1954).

Maslow's message for the beginning speaker—as well as for the teacher of the beginning speech course—is clear: *The need to express and to communicate must be stronger than the need for safety if the speaker is to be effective.* In the case of John Thatch, the psychological threat of facing an audience was so severe that not even the inducement of the class vice-presidency could overcome his fear.

the danger of trying to hide

The problem of psychological safety is no small matter. At some time or another, most of us have been urged into situations we find disagreeable by well-meaning friends who assure us, "Go ahead, it won't kill you." This, often as not, is little consolation, for, as comedian Alan King has astutely observed, "Most of us would rather die than make a fool of ourselves." How else can we explain, for example, that, in a speech course, some otherwise good students will perform every other assignment but will consistently miss class on the days they are assigned to speak, even at the risk of failing the course?

An example of this avoidance reaction is provided by a neighbor and colleague of ours—a young math professor at the University of Kansas. Although a good teacher, intelligent, and socially inclined, he's convinced that he can't speak in public. This is true in spite of the fact that he lectures regularly to his classes. In fact, he has such an aversion to public speaking that, as he has often declared, he would not have attended his alma mater, the University of Washington—a school he dearly loves—if it had required that he enroll in a speech course. It is paradoxical that he expressed this opinion even while affirming the need for, and approving through his vote, speech instruction for all College of Arts and Science students at the University of Kansas.

Although we may—as does our friend the math teacher—acknowledge the irrationality of our apprehensions about public speaking, this, for most of us, does little to alleviate the condition. As one speech text expresses it, "every new audience, every new listener is an unknown, and the unknown often is colored more or less with threat. Accordingly, when the beginning speaker confronts such a situation he tends to recoil from the threatening audience contact, refusing to look at the listeners, and exposing as little of himself as possible."[6]

Whether we like it or not, we become the center of attention when we take our place on the platform. Although in this capacity we are examined and evaluated by our listeners, it is hardly ever with the intensity and malevolent ill-will so often imagined by the novice speaker. Furthermore, the inevitable exposure that takes place when a speaker confronts an audience can become a significant asset to him rather than a detriment. As Charles T. Brown and Charles Van Riper point out:

> We who speak must accept assessment by our listeners as a matter of course, and not be traumatized by it. Indeed, the greatest potential value in public speaking is this training in the sharpening of one's awareness of his identity. The good speaker meets the challenge and hears a silent trumpet that brings out his best. There are some, of course, who pretend that no horn has sounded, who almost deny that they have listeners, who speak only to those enchanted listeners—themselves. These people rarely speak well, and they do not communicate, even though thereby they hide their essential fear. There are others who try to flee the challenge, avoiding any sort of speaking situation where their impoverished egos may be displayed. But life lies in wait for these escapists. Only the hermit in the Ozarks or the Trappist monk with his eternal vow of silence can hope to avoid successfully all demands for speech before some scanning listener. If we run away we do so at our peril, for avoidance begets fear and fear in turn more avoidance.[7]

[6] Charles T. Brown and Charles Van Riper, *Speech and Man* (Englewood Cliffs, N.J.: Prentice-Hall, © 1966), p. 47.

[7] Brown and Van Riper, p. 44.

Avoidance, developed as a response to the threat of speaking situations, involves consequences far more severe than the simple decision that one can live quite comfortably outside the public spotlight. One authority testifies that eventually such a person tends "to avoid interactions rather than participate. He knows that he does not react as others do in personalized communicative situations. This awareness often pushes him to seek occupations and activities that will spare him from communicating, where his peers choose such activities on a basis of interest or commitment without much concern for the communicative requirements."[8] Our friend the math professor, for example, tells us it is not uncommon for him to avoid expressing his opinions during faculty meetings, even when he feels rather strongly about the issue being discussed.

If depriving associates of your best ideas were the only consequence of the avoidance habit, it would be bad enough. The ramifications, however, go much further—they reflect upon your personal character and competence. If you consistently refrain from expressing your ideas, people with whom you come into contact will eventually begin to suspect that you have none. This is as true in the classroom as in the business office. Those who associate with such a person "may describe him," Gerald M. Phillips attests, "as 'tight-lipped,' 'curt,' 'pauciloquent,' 'uncommunicative,' 'shifty,' 'recondite,' 'withdrawn,' 'close-mouthed,' 'shy,' 'diffident,' 'fearful,' 'apprehensive,' 'antisocial,' 'schizophrenic,' and apply many other adjectives which imply denigration."[9]

practice makes good and good makes confident

Most of us realize the desirability and virtual inevitability of face-to-face communication—including public speaking—and make some effort to become proficient. Although most of us

[8] Gerald M. Phillips, "Reticence: Pathology of the Normal Speaker," *Speech Monographs*, Vol. 35 (March 1968), p. 40.

[9] Phillips, p. 40.

would, if we could, develop such proficiency in the privacy of our own homes, this is just not possible. To develop skill and confidence in public speaking, one must have experience with real audiences. Only through this approach are we able to learn the personal satisfaction and sense of accomplishment that results from presenting a good speech.

Ideally, our first experiences with real audiences will come in a well-instructed public speaking course. Here we are able "to introduce ourselves intimately to a group of our fellow human beings and to understand the dynamics of that confrontation. Here we have the freedom to expose and explore ourselves in relative safety since all others are equally challenged in the same way."[10] The classroom should provide the learner with an environment in which the threat of public speaking is minimized while, at the same time, the speaker is stimulated to discover and talk about things that really make a difference.

Most readers of this book, we assume, will be using it as part of a course in speech. Whether or not it is used as an adjunct to a formal course, its purpose is the same—to enable you to produce the kind of public speech that will provide a meaningful experience for both you and your listeners.

talking with friends

Contributing to the constraint one feels when asked to make a speech must be the feeling that "making a speech"—talking to an audience—is somehow different from sitting down and conversing with one's friends. One feels that there is a special art or a particular set of requirements which belongs to speechmaking and which doesn't apply to good conversation with friends. Since making a speech is something different from talking to one's friends, one immediately sets up this emotional hurdle to the business of making a speech.

[10] Brown and Van Riper, *Speech and Man*, p. 45.

Our contention, to the contrary, is that making a speech is not greatly different from talking to one's friends. In fact, to speak well—to make a good public speech—requires very many of the same attitudes and the same kinds of behavior that occur when you sit down to have a conversation with someone you enjoy talking to. We think that underneath every good public speech rests an attitude of trust in the audience, as if the speaker conveys to the audience, whom he may or may not have seen before, "You people are my friends and I'd like to sit down and talk to you, only since there are so many of you, I'll stand up instead."

A colleague of ours tells a story that illustrates how trusting an audience can pay off:

> I had a student in class one semester who was the only speaker to get spontaneous applause from the rest of the class. You know how he got it? He got it by making a stupid error—not simply by making the error, but by the fact he trusted his audience.
>
> He did this very foolish thing of ending his speech with a quotation he had memorized. Now, it's all right to memorize a quotation, but if you go up to give that speech without the quotation on a note card or written on your cuff, this is taking a chance. So he came to the end of a pretty good speech and said, "I'd like to conclude in the words of George Washington." Then everything went blank, and he just stood there.
>
> There was that breathless moment while we watched for him to begin to tremble and sweat and become uncomfortable. Instead, he smiled cheerfully and said, "I seem to have forgotten the words of George Washington, but if you'll wait just a minute I'll go back to my desk and get them." He ambled back to his desk, got his notebook, came back up to the front, smiled again, and said, "Now, in the words of George Washington," and then he read the quotation and the audience all cheered.

Why did the audience cheer this speaker? Certainly not because he did such a spectacularly intelligent thing in forgetting his quotation. They cheered because the speaker had trusted them. He had said to them through his behavior, "You're my friends; I've gotten myself into a little bind here, but I know you'll wait until I can work my way out of it." You can count on this kind of relationship from an audience, and it illustrates that the line we tend to draw between conversation and public speaking is not a reasonable one.

preparing your "conversation"

A public speech differs from just plain conversation in that one has time, when planning a public speech, to prepare himself to talk better than he would talk if he were sitting down at the dinner table conversing with a friend. In one sense, it's really easier to do well in a public speech than it is to do well in a conversation because the conversation, which may seem so easy, occurs spontaneously without time for preparation. The speech which may seem so hard, however, is just a conversation we've had time to think through. We've had time to prepare ourselves; we've had time to plan what we're going to say. Consequently, it ought to be better and ought to be more fun than the conversation.

In the next few pages, we're going to talk about this business of planning time. Suppose you were asked to prepare a speech (and we imagine, if you're in a speech class, that you either have been or will be asked shortly); what should you start doing when you know that you have this speech to make? How do you make use of your time?

One of the most destructive things you can do is to start worrying about the whole matter, saying to yourself: "Next Tuesday I have to give a speech; my gosh, this is terrific pressure! I wish I were on Wednesday instead of Tuesday, or, better yet, Thursday. I never feel well on Tuesday. As a matter of fact, with a little luck, I may have a severe cold next Tuesday and I won't be here at all." If you start on this kind of activity, you can fill the entire period between the time when you know you have to make a speech and the time when the speech occurs with a whole lot of evasive action. Every time you think about the speech then postpone its preparation, you're undercutting yourself; you're building the job into one of greater proportions than it actually constitutes.

Let's hypothesize a speaking situation. Let's assume that a college student, employed as a part-time group worker in a home for delinquent boys, has been asked to make a speech about juvenile group work to the local Lions Club. Just to give him a name, we'll call our speaker Joe College. Under some pressure, Joe accepts this speaking assignment and faces up to the fact that just as surely as the clock marches on, he will have to appear and talk about his work to the Lions Club.

If Joe is sensible, he won't spend any time saying that he has a headache or that there likely will be a crisis in the community which will cause the meeting to be adjourned or that maybe nuclear warfare will break out and the whole thing will be forgotten. Rather, Joe will settle down and get to work immediately on the task of preparing his speech.

Getting to work is something he can do just by thinking, just by sitting and beginning to talk to himself internally about what he is going to say to his audience.

We're going to carry you through the steps that Joe pursues as he works purposefully toward the development of his speech. In doing so, we will try to boil down the whole business of speech preparation into six simple, but important, steps—the kinds of decisions Joe will have to make to get himself ready to do a good job with his speech.

decision 1: the central idea

About the first thing Joe must ask himself is the question "What am I going to talk about?" Further, he must try to narrow down that topic to something we call in speechmaking a central idea. It isn't enough that he have a title for his talk. He can't simply say, "I'm going to talk about juvenile delinquency" or "I'm going to talk about the job of the group worker." He has to answer the question "What is it that I want to say to this audience?" or "What's the central thing I want to tell them?" Unless Joe has a statement, or a central idea, he doesn't really have a workable purpose in mind. So Joe starts looking right away for his central idea.

In many ways, an audience knows it's going to hear a good speech if it hears a man who, in one way or another, stands up in front and says, "I have something to say to you people, and what I want to say is this . . ." If a speaker has come to the point where he wants to say something to his audience and works out a sentence or two that says it, you know right away that he came prepared to talk—that he has a message, that he has worked out that message, has thought it through, and is convinced that this is what he wants to say. So Joe talks to himself—"What is it I want to say?"—until he comes up with the central idea that he wants to put across to his audience. This idea of relevance—from the perspectives of both speaker and audience—is discussed at length in Chapter 2.

In this case, Joe decides that he does have a purpose and that his particular purpose is to get this audience to believe in the need for specialized training for people who work with juvenile offenders. He thinks that the job requires specialized training, and he wants to get the audience to accept this idea. So Joe says to himself, "My central idea is going to be to tell this audience as clearly as I can that there is a need for specialized training for those people who work with juvenile offenders." Or he might word it differently: "We need specialists to serve as group workers in our juvenile correctional institutions."

Once he has picked out his central idea, Joe must think of a way he can get into it during the speech. So he says to himself, "Actually, when I say we need specialized training for juvenile group workers, I'm going to have to answer a question for this audience—I'm going to have to tell them why. My speech really will consist of an answer to a question. It has a central idea which will answer the question 'Why do we need specialists?'"

At this point, Joe thinks he's doing pretty well. He says, "If I

the speaker as "number one"

17

can state this question, 'Why do we need specialists to work with juvenile offenders?' and if I can answer it in an interesting and persuasive way, then my audience should be prepared to accept the idea that we do need specialists." In other words, he will have gotten his message across and he will have achieved his purpose.

decision 2: audience interest

Now that he has figured out what he wants to talk about, Joe is ready to step back and ask how he is going to get into this central idea. The question he is raising with himself here is concerned basically with how he is going to interest his audience, a problem to which Chapter 4 is devoted in its entirety.

If Joe can't think of any other way to interest his audience, there are lots worse ways of starting a speech than getting up and saying:

> Friends, I have something I want to tell you. I want to tell you that we need people with specialized training to deal with juvenile lawbreakers. Now, I know that when I make that statement you're going to raise some questions. You're going to say, "Why do we need specialists to deal with juveniles?" That's why I'm here today—I'm here to answer the question, "Why do we need specialists in this field?" and I'm going to answer that question by telling you . . .

In this way Joe is off into his speech. In other words, if he can't think of any other way to start his speech than just standing up and saying to his audience, "I'll tell you what I'm going to tell you," then begin talking, he could do much worse. A speaker who hits directly and quickly into the purpose of his speech is a person who often gets a good deal of respect from his audience.

On the other hand, Joe could approach his subject with a bit more flourish. Joe knows that a lot of people are hard to wake up. With their own problems on their minds, they frequently tend to be somewhat disinterested in listening to what a speaker is going to say. It might be better, therefore, if Joe could think of some special way to interest his audience.

How can a speaker interest an audience? There are a number of ways, as Chapter 4 points out, but one of the easiest is to tell your audience a story. Thus, many successful speakers start out with an anecdote, or story, that relates somehow to the central idea, or purpose, of their speech. As a matter of fact, it is often a good idea to leave this part of one's speech preparation until the very last. Although, understandably, Joe concerned himself with the problem immediately upon having settled on a central idea, it is often easier to delay making a specific decision about how to devise an interesting opening. Later, one can go back through his speech and pick out the most interesting piece of information or story in the entire speech and pull it out to use at the beginning of the speech. Even though the material that is transferred to the introduction will have to be replaced, it will help the speaker get off to an interesting start.

What do we mean by a story that interests people? The following example illustrates nicely what an interesting story is like. It was told by a former professor of ours to a group of police officers.

This is a story about a boy named Sunshine Smith. Now, Sunshine was an interesting young man. He was an eighth grader who lived in Washington, D.C., and who got into trouble with the law. The nature of his trouble was quite exciting. It seems that Sunshine had worked out a rather crisp, clear, well-planned business operation. He was operating, in his particular school, a kind of business which provided both full satisfaction for value received and which enabled him to collect quite a little money each week. What he was doing was selling protection; he was selling protection to the seventh and eighth graders in his school. He was selling it for ten cents a week, and he had a very large list of subscribers.

Now, if you're going to sell anything, you've got to motivate the people you're going to sell to, and Sunshine had worked out fairly good motivation. For one thing, he was stronger than almost anybody else in the seventh and eighth grades in his school, a little larger, and he could run faster. For another thing, he had a very fine switchblade knife. As a result of the fact that he was bigger, and stronger, and could run faster, and had a knife, he was able to demonstrate that the other boys needed protection. So, he provided the motivation. Obviously, since he was the man furnishing the threat, he was also the best man to provide protection. Thus, as I said, he gave value received—for ten cents a week he guaranteed the safety of everyone in that school from Sunshine. Unfortunately, as happens to so many entrepreneurs, Sunshine came unfavorably to the attention of the law and they arrested him. This broke up the business.

Well now, the interesting thing about this case is, "Why was Sunshine in this business?" And when you start looking into this, you begin to uncover some rather interesting things. Sunshine was in the eighth grade but was reading at about the second grade level. He didn't read very well. He was in the eighth grade but his writing was pretty retarded. He didn't write particularly well. Now, if you ask what kind of success can Sunshine achieve in this school, I think your answer is going to have to be, "Very, very limited success." A boy who can't read particularly well, and who can't write particularly well, who's in the eighth grade, is one who is not going to star particularly in class. When questions are asked he's not likely to be the one who has the answers, he's not going to get much favorable attention from others on the basis of what he can accomplish in the classroom.

Well, this isn't necessarily so bad if he can walk home at night and feel pretty secure in the kind of environment he finds there. But for young Mr. Smith the possibility of walking home and feeling secure was rather limited, too. His father was seldom there, because he spent most of his time as an involuntary ward of the police department. He didn't spend a great deal of time outside jail. His mother eked out a living, but the living she eked out was tied to a very ancient, but not particularly honorable, profession known as prostitution. So she wasn't home very often either, although she did provide a little support for the family occasionally.

We can see Sunshine, who hasn't performed very well in school and hasn't received much credit, walking home to receive support, and credit, and security. What's he going to do? Is he going to walk back to the neighborhood and say: "How do you do, I'm Sunshine Smith. You know, a member of the Smith family, we live down on the corner. Father's in jail and mother's out prostituting at the moment, but all of you know who I am"? Not precisely! This boy doesn't have much security in the kind of environment he's got set up for himself.

So we're looking at a young man who is just like every other adolescent in certain respects. He's just like every other adolescent in the fact that he wants to have identity, that he wants to be someone, that he wants other people to look at him and say, "We know who you are, we acknowledge you, and we respect you." He wants to have his place in the sun, in other words, just like every other young person does. But he's got a pretty hard proposition knowing how he's going to get it. He isn't going to get his place in the sun in the classroom, he isn't going to get it at home, he isn't going to get it in his neighborhood. How is he going to get it?

Now, if you look at this situation, I would submit that you would have to say to yourself that young Mr. Smith worked out a rather ingenious, and rather logical, kind of activity to engage in. He didn't have many assets, but he had a few. He was bigger, he was stronger, he could run faster, and he was more desperate—*he was more desperate*—than almost anybody else in his grade. And he put those together, and he developed this little racket which got him the unfavorable attention of the law and caused him to be taken off to jail, although he was ultimately paroled, in this particular instance, and put on a kind of rehabilitation program.

Now this is Sunshine's story, and the only thing I'm trying to illustrate when I tell this story is the fact that when we look at a juvenile offender, or a kid who has gotten into trouble, we're not looking at a boy who differs fundamentally from other boys. We're looking at a boy who wants the same things, who goes after the same kinds of goals, but circum-

the speaker as "number one"

stance constrains or restricts the way he can get his recognition, the way he can make his mark, the way he can achieve status.[11]

That's the story of Sunshine Smith. Not only does it demonstrate how an idea can be made interesting, but it is also appropriate to the subject about which Joe College, our speaker, is preparing to give his talk to the Lions Club. Joe could tell this story, or something like it, and he would have interested his audience in the subject of juvenile delinquency and in the problems of the kinds of young people he works with at the juvenile home.

We suspect that Joe, like every one of you reading this book, has within him ten, twenty, thirty, forty, fifty stories—true stories, real events that have happened to him and which, because they have some pathos, some human interest, some excitement, some drama in them, he could use in his speech and which his audience would be interested in hearing. Out of this fund of experience, each of us has many, many ways of approaching other people and talking to them in a way which would interest them. All we need to do is look for it, dig for it inside our own experience, then relate it to the kind of message we want to get across to an audience.

decision 3: getting from one point to the next

Joe decides he is going to start off by telling the story of Sunshine Smith. But having told that story, how does he get from his human-interest introduction into his central idea? Well, he needs some kind of a bridge, obviously. He wants to tell the story, then he wants to find a device that leads into his central idea. Determining what that bridge will be is often a rather easy matter; sometimes it only requires a single sentence. The question Joe asks himself is this: "When I've said this, and the next thing I want to say is that, how do I get from

[11] This illustration, as well as some of the ideas contained in the last section of this chapter, were derived from a speech delivered by Donald K. Smith at the University of Minnesota in the summer of 1963.

here to there?" This, in speech terminology, is called working out a transition. Transitions, along with other methods for achieving clarity, will be covered in more detail in Chapter 3.

Joe, who has decided that he will begin his speech with a story of a young man in trouble, works out his transition like this:

> Some young people are always in trouble. The real question is "Do young people in trouble need special help with their troubles? Is there anything about the difficulties of the young that seem to call for special help?" Today, I'm going to answer that question for you. I'm going to ask the question "Why do we need specially trained help for young people who are in trouble?" and then I'm going to try to answer that question.

decision 4: limiting your answer

If Joe is wise, his answer will be limited to two or three points, never more than five, in a relatively short speech. One of the problems most of us get into when we make speeches is to try to cover too many points while saying too little about each one. Good advice is to make just two or three points for an audience, but to make those points very clearly and in a way the audience won't forget.

With this advice in mind, Joe says, "I'm going to give two answers to the question, 'Why do we need specialists?' I'm going to give an old answer and I'm going to give a new answer. When I've given these two answers I think that most of you will believe that the problems of the young require rather specialized attention."

In approaching the "old answer" to his question, Joe decides that the oldest answer in the world to this question is the fact that growing up is the hardest job that any of us ever perform. In order to prove this, Joe decides that he will tell the audience another story. Perhaps he will tell them the story of Jimmy Whitmore, one of his boys at the school, and the trouble he had growing up. Or perhaps Joe will decide to tell them a personal experience, some of the problems he had as an adolescent in trying to reach maturity. This is going to be Joe's old reason: "Growing up is the hardest job in the world and nobody is ever in greater need of help, specialized and intelligent help, than at that period of his life when he is trying to become an adult but doesn't quite know how."

Next, Joe asks in transition, "What's the new reason why we need specialists to work with young people in trouble?" The "new reason," Joe decides, is that the young people today are growing up in a quite different world from the one that adults grew up in. The mobility provided by the easy availability of the automobile and the pressures toward material acquisition provided by advertising and the mass media are only two of the many problems faced by young people in this increasingly complex world.

decision 5: developing an idea

Obviously, Joe can't give examples of all the problems faced by the young in today's society, but he will want to find one or two anecdotes to illustrate the point that the world has changed. In addition to illustrating his contention, however, Joe may wish to include some other kinds of evidence in support of his point. Although the process of enhancing the believability of an idea will be discussed more thoroughly in Chapter 5, we can say something about the problem now. One of the things that Joe would like to do for his audience, besides talking to them from his own firsthand experience, is to provide them with some information, or data, that many of them perhaps did not know before. He may, for example, decide to substantiate his contention concerning the difficulties of growing up in contemporary society by telling his listeners about, or even reading a quotation from, a book he has just read by the journalist Dan Wakefield. The following section from the book, Joe thinks, would be just the thing to provide some verification for his views:

In this society they are taunted by not having all the best, the latest sleek car and fine mink lounging pajamas and color TV's and washing machines and all of the incredible effluvia of the cornucopia filled by the richest country in the history of the world. You see how "the other half lives"; in fact, you are taken into the very living rooms of the rich and powerful by the magic of television, and the ads you see say that the wonderful products offered, the luxury vacations in Caribbean islands, the mighty new automobiles, the sleek, jeweled women are for *you*, Mr. Viewer, not just the lords, but all of you out there in videoland.[12]

Statistical information offers another source of supporting material from which Joe can draw. In this particular case, the kind of information he would probably want to bring to his audience would be the latest and best data he can get concerning the scope of juvenile delinquency in their community or state, or perhaps in the nation at large in comparison with their community or state. He wants to show them that he's not only talking about the world of Sunshine Smith or Jimmy Whitmore, but that he's talking about a problem that affects a large number of young people.

Now, Joe has just about got his speech prepared. He started out to find a relevant central idea, he figured out a way to make that idea clear and interesting to his audience, he worked out a series of transitions, he devised two main points to support his central idea, and he developed those points with examples, quotations, and statistics.

decision 6: "talking out" the speech

Looking over what he has prepared, Joe is convinced that it's going to make a pretty good speech. So he says, "I'll write it out and I'll memorize it." But if Joe starts writing this speech out in order to either read it or memorize it, he's

---

[12] Dan Wakefield, *Supernation at Peace and War* (Boston: Little, Brown and Co., 1968), p. 80.

making a big mistake. He should say, "I'll talk it out until I know I can talk it."

To begin with, Joe should equip himself with a brief outline. In this particular case, he could probably get his outline on just one or two note cards. In fact, it might not be much more than this:

I. Introduction: Sunshine Smith story

II. Main idea: Why do we need more and better trained specialists to work with young people in trouble?
  A. Old reason: Growing up is the most difficult job anyone faces.
    1. Jimmy Whitmore story
    2. Personal example
  B. New reason: Contemporary society poses many new problems for the young.
    1. Examples of problems in contemporary society
    2. Quotation from Dan Wakefield's book
    3. Statistics about the scope of juvenile delinquency

III. Conclusion: We do need more and better trained specialists to work with young people in trouble.

Once Joe gets his outline down on a card or two he should find some place to practice where, if at all possible, he can talk out loud. If he can't find a place to talk out loud, he can always mumble to himself. This may sound funny, but it's important that Joe have a chance to practice actually verbalizing his speech. He must have a chance to *say* what he's going to say rather than just thinking it. He must talk his speech through until it feels good—until the ideas, and the words that express those ideas, come easily and naturally. This may require talking the speech through only once, or it may require a dozen practice sessions. The important thing is that Joe, or anyone else, should talk through his speech until he knows that he can tell his story to his audience. This knowledge will go a long way toward instilling the kind of confidence we all would like when facing an audience.

In the following chapters we will discuss in detail the problems Joe faced in the preparation of his speech. To achieve success as a speaker one must be relevant, clear, interesting, and believable, and he must know how to incorporate all of these factors into a single speech. These are the subjects that we will consider during the remainder of the book.

2

be relevant

The quality of relevance, as we view it, is the first criterion of a successful public speech. But what is relevant to any given person is a function, not only of his own idiosyncrasies, but also of the general values and character of the time in which he lives. This "social mind," as historian Stow Persons calls it, "is the cluster of ideas and attitudes that gives to a society whatever uniqueness or individuality it may have as an epoch in the history of thought."[1]

Although it is difficult to judge from such close perspective, there are signs that we are entering a period which may well be described as an *age of awareness*—a time of individual concern and social activism. And of particular meaning to us is that in such an age the role of communication in general, and public speaking in particular, is destined to become one of unique importance.

the temper of our time

No one can deny that things are changing. In fact, says Eric Hoffer, from whose book we borrowed the title for this section, "It is my assumption that the main difficulty and challenge of our age is drastic change. . . . It is becoming evident that, no

[1] Stow Persons, *American Minds* (New York: Holt, Rinehart and Winston, 1958), p. vii.

matter how desirable, drastic change is the most difficult and dangerous experience mankind has undergone."[2]

There is no question that the significant social changes now occurring in our nation have been accompanied—and, perhaps, in part caused—by protest, demonstration, and riot. But although this violent aspect of contemporary society has received extensive comment, it is neither the only dimension of our changing culture, nor is it, in our opinion, the most important. From our point of view, the singularly significant characteristic of our time is the developing sensitivity among all levels of the population to the nation's and the world's social problems, and the increasing disposition of the people—especially the young—to become personally involved in solutions to these problems.

speaking changes, too

Accompanying these changes in our social values has been a comparable change in the role and importance of the public speaker. Although speechmaking seems inherently associated with the process of problem solving, there have been significant periods in the history of western culture when public speech has occupied a position substantially divorced from any meaningful discussion of social issues. Sometimes the condition has resulted from totalitarian governments restricting the involvement of its citizens. For a period of more than three hundred years during the Roman Empire, for example, the predominant role of public speech was reduced to that of display—its only purpose to demonstrate the speaker's cleverness and to provide entertainment for the audience. At other times, the demise of speechmaking has simply reflected the values and tastes of the time. Thus, there have been periods—some

[2] Eric Hoffer, *The Temper of Our Time* (New York: Harper & Row, 1964), p. xi.

not so very long ago—when nicety of language, indirection, and circumlocution have been considered the hallmarks of successful speaking.

The prevailing mood today seems to be one of growing impatience—in the face of urgent social needs—with these characteristics of the old rhetoric. "A rhetorical theory suitable to our age must," according to Robert L. Scott and Donald K. Smith, "take into account the charge that civility and decorum serve as masks for the preservation of injustices, that they condemn the dispossessed to non-being, and that as transmitted in a technological society, they become the instrumentalities of power for those who 'have.' "[3]

Although the tendency of this "new rhetoric" thus far has been "aggressive, abrasive, non-conciliatory, even shocking, and apparently unconcerned with making adaptations to the mores or sensitivities of its audience,"[4] we would argue that these tendencies are neither necessary nor desirable characteristics of public speaking in most instances. Just as we contended earlier that violence is not the prime dimension of contemporary culture, we now contend that bad manners are not integral to a relevant and effective contemporary rhetoric.

What is criterial to relevant dialogue in our time, as we perceive it, is the growing disposition of our people to see it, hear it, and tell it "like it is." As with the Greeks of ancient Athens, we are approaching a society that seeks to repudiate

[3] Robert L. Scott and Donald K. Smith, "The Rhetoric of Confrontation," *Quarterly Journal of Speech*, Vol. 55 (February 1969), p. 8.

[4] Franklyn S. Haiman, "The Rhetoric of 1968: A Farewell to Rational Discourse," in *The Ethics of Controversy: Politics and Protest*, Proceedings of the First Annual Symposium on Issues in Public Communication, eds. Donn W. Parson and Wil A. Linkugel (Lawrence: University of Kansas, 1968), p. 128.

its "vital lies."[5] For the Greeks, as Edith Hamilton writes, this included the rejection of such romantic myths as held by the later Romans that it was sweet to die for one's country. It may, on occasion, be necessary, the Athenian would admit, but it is never sweet.[6] For Americans of the latter part of the twentieth century, "telling it like it is" includes the rejection of the idea that black males really feel more comfortable when treated like errant children; that the poor wouldn't know what to do with the good things of life anyway; that the young are old enough to die fighting for their country but not old enough to intelligently govern their own affairs.

One good indication of the rhetorical temper of our time, we think, is reflected in the spreading popularity of what has come to be called Soul music.

> Soul music is sincerity, a homely distillation of everybody's daily portion of pain and joy. "It pulls the cover off," explains Jim Stewart, a former banker and country fiddler. . . . "It's not the moon in June. It's life. . . ." The difference between Tin Pan Alley and Soul is not hard to define. A conventional tunesmith might write: "You're still near, my darling, though we're apart/ I'll hold you always in my heart." The soul singer might put it: "Baby, since you split the scene the rent's come due/ Without you or your money, it's hard, yeah, hard to be true."[7]

There's a growing inclination for us to want the truth, even when it's unpleasant. The Presidential campaign of 1968 illustrates the point. Third-party candidate, George Wallace, though he was perceived by most Negroes as an antagonist, was sometimes preferred by them to the two major-party candidates. Former heavyweight boxing champion, Cassius Clay (Muhammad Ali) put it this way: "I admire the man. He tells the truth,

---

[5] Edith Hamilton, *The Greek Way* (New York: New American Library, 1948), p. 75.

[6] Hamilton, p. 75.

[7] *Time*, June 28, 1968, p. 62.

a time to speak

and he don't beat around the bush."[8] Clay's position was seconded by black leader Adam Clayton Powell, who asserted during a television interview, "I commend George Wallace, even though I disagree with him 100 percent. He's the only man out there that's got guts."[9]

Until recently, and perhaps even now, some speech theory books have advised that speakers facing audiences hostile to their cause should proceed only through suggestion and indirection. Even disregarding the ethical considerations of such evasiveness, this seems to us, considering the times in which we live, to be bad advice. It's unlikely, we think, that in any ordinary circumstance a speaker could approach an audience in such a way that he could win approval of his proposition while still concealing it from the listeners. People today are too well informed for a speaker to get by with the kind of equivocation that perhaps was once possible. Such a speaker is destined to win for himself only disdain and ridicule.

Today's realistic speaker acknowledges that a speech can accomplish only so much in altering the attitudes of a hostile audience. He knows that an honest, direct approach (though probably not an abusive or insulting one) will accomplish as much as it is possible to accomplish when he confronts antagonistic listeners. One of the best examples of this approach that we've come across was provided by evangelist Billy Graham in a convocation speech at the University of Minnesota:

In trying to decide what I should talk to you about today, I could not help but remember that a few months ago I was in Toronto. And I was invited to the Empire Club, which is made up of a thousand of the leading industrialists of the Dominion of Canada. Their speaker that day was Walter Reuther, the American labor leader. I was invited to sit beside him at the head table. He had just called a strike outside of Toronto in all the General Motors plants, and it was a very unpopular

[8] *Time*, October 4, 1968, p. 44.

[9] Interview, WDAF-TV, Kansas City, Mo., October 10, 1968.

strike. And I wondered what he was going to say, because I could sense the hostility in the audience.

They introduced him, they applauded him politely, and he stood up. And he said, "I think all of you would like to know what labor thinks; what labor believes. I know that most of you will not agree with what I'm going to say today. But," he said, "I'm going to lay the cards on the table."

For thirty minutes he gave those men a message, the likes of which I've never heard. I don't think anybody in the room agreed altogether with him, but when he finished they gave him one of the greatest standing ovations I've ever heard because they appreciated his candor and his frankness.

Now, I know that all of you are not going to agree with what I'm going to say today. But I think all of us are disturbed about the times in which we live. And I think all of us are searching and questing for answers to the dilemmas and the problems with which all of us are faced. And the answer that I give today I know is only one answer, and I know that this answer is controversial. I know that it's debatable. But I want to present it, because to me it is *the* answer, and I'm fully convinced that there is no other answer to the dilemmas that face the human race at this hour.

In this introduction to his speech, Dr. Graham not only illustrates the effectiveness of candor, even when confronting a hostile audience, but also demonstrates the use of analogy—a point we will discuss further in Chapter 5.

We live, without doubt, in a time of change—a time when our old institutions and our traditionally most cherished values are, on every hand, being questioned and attacked. "We are discovering," Hoffer tells us, "that broken habits can be more painful and crippling than broken bones, and that disintegrating values may have as deadly a fallout as disintegrating atoms."[10] Yet, the temper of our time is also an optimistic one, for we live in an age of unparalleled concern for the problems of society and willingness to confront these problems honestly and directly.

[10] Hoffer, *Temper of Our Time*, p. xi.

During such an age the public speaker has the opportunity to assume a more meaningful role than at any other period of history. For it is the speaker, or "rhetor," as Lloyd Bitzer calls him, who "alters reality by bringing into existence a discourse of such a character that the audience, in thought and action, is so engaged that it becomes mediator of change."[11] It is within this context, therefore, that we move on to discuss further the idea of relevance as it relates directly to both the speaker and his audience.

relevance and the self

There is perhaps no word more prominent on the campuses of our nation than "relevant." Concerned students challenge all aspects of the academic environment—curriculum, faculty, grades, administrative procedures—on the grounds of relevancy. They organize their own "free universities," and in some areas even "free high schools," in order to provide courses which they feel are relevant to their interests.

In the face of this concern for relevance, it is both ironical and puzzling that students, when faced by the need to speak publicly, seem so often to run for the *Reader's Digest* or some other source of ready-made ideas. There appears to be a prevailing attitude that good speeches start with someone else's ideas, and that these, in turn, can be discovered through the library's card catalog or the *Readers' Guide to Periodical Literature*. This, we submit, is an obvious defense mechanism which, more than any other single cause, is the reason why so many speeches—both in and out of the classroom—are superficial and stultifying. How can they be anything else when the speaker hides behind a manuscript full of words that have no meaningful relationship to his real self?

Wayne Booth, an English professor at the University of

[11] Lloyd Bitzer, "The Rhetorical Situation," *Philosophy and Rhetoric*, Vol. 1 (January 1968), p. 4.

Chicago, tells a story about one of his early teaching experiences that we think gets to the very heart of the problem of relevancy. Actually, almost any speech or English teacher could tell a hundred stories just like it.

In my first year of teaching I taught a whole unit on "exposition" without ever suggesting, so far as I can remember, that the students ask themselves what their expositions were *for*. So they wrote expositions like this one: . . . the title is "Family Relationships in More's *Utopia*." "In this theme I would like to discuss some of the relationships with the family which Thomas More elaborates and sets forth in his book, *Utopia*. The first thing that I would like to discuss about family relations is that overpopulation, according to More, is a just cause of war." And so on. Can you hear that student sneering at me, in his opening? What he is saying is something like "you ask for a meaningless paper, I give you a meaningless paper." He knows that he has no audience except me. He knows that I don't want to read his summary of family relations in *Utopia*, and he knows that I know that he therefore has no rhetorical purpose. Because he has not been led to see a question which he considers worth answering, or an audience that could possibly care one way or the other, the paper is worse than no paper at all, even though it has no grammatical or spelling errors and is organized right down the line, one, two, three."[12]

As Booth's example makes clear, there is no such thing as an intrinsically "good" idea. Ideas, and the words used to express them, are good or vital or significant because they are perceived as such by a particular person in a particular circumstance. In other words, ideas must be evaluated in terms of people, and when the context involves public speech, *the person who must be considered first is the speaker himself*. It is

[12] Wayne C. Booth, "The Rhetorical Stance," *Toward a New Rhetoric* (Papers from the 1963 Conference on College Composition and Communication), p. 4.

axiomatic that none of us is going to subject himself to the risk involved—to the kind of commitment required—in public speech unless *first* the reason for speaking is important enough to us personally that it overcomes whatever threat the speaking situation constitutes to our psychological safety. As speakers in quest of relevance, therefore, our first look should be, not in the library, but into ourselves—our needs, our values, our goals. Research, of course, can be an aid to both the germination and the development of our ideas, but it cannot in itself provide anyone with a single meaningful idea.

What makes the difference, a journalist writes of Soul singer Aretha Franklin, is more than a matter of technique:

> It is her fierce, gritty conviction. . . . She does not seem to be performing so much as bearing witness to a reality so simple and compelling that she could not possibly fake it. In her selection of songs . . . she unfailingly opts for those that frame her own view of life. "If a song's about something I've experienced or that could've happened to me, it's good," she says. "But if it's alien to me, I couldn't lend anything to it."[13]

discovery—the self and the idea

An item in the local paper caught our attention recently because it seemed to epitomize that old journalistic axiom that news is not when "dog bites man," but when "man bites dog." This story reported a rather dramatic reversal in the current trend of liberal college students rebelling against what they see as their more conservative administrations. In telling how the conservative students of a small Kentucky college were protesting against the liberalism of their young president, the paper quoted one sophomore as saying, "He keeps telling us to do our own thing, but we don't know what our own thing is, and even if we did, we wouldn't know how to do it."

It should be clear to anyone—student or teacher—who has

---

[13] *Time*, June 28, 1968, p. 62.

sat through the drivel and dreariness that characterize so much public speaking, that most speakers either have no notion of the need for personal involvement with the ideas they express, or they have no real insight into who they are or what is important to them.

Does it have to be this way? Are there people who by nature are so lacking in depth that nothing will ever really make a difference to them? Perhaps we're overly optimistic, but we think not. We think that simply being human—that quality common to all of us—is enough if we can only become conscious of what our humanity really means. Georges Gusdorf says it this way: "A living man, writer or not, always has something to say, as a contribution to the reality of the world in which his task is to declare himself."[14]

man is not a cauliflower

"Man," writes Jean-Paul Sartre, "is nothing else but what he makes of himself. . . . Man is at the start a plan which is aware of itself, rather than a patch of moss, a piece of garbage, or a cauliflower."[15]

Fortunately, we live in a society in which the process of increasing one's self-awareness is enhanced. Thus, *Time* magazine commented in an essay on the role of the activist in American society:

As a nation built on the right to dissent, the U.S. still cherishes the qualities of initiative, self-sufficiency and independence that embellish every page of its history. The prevailing political climate has always encouraged the Doer's growth. But even in today's permissive culture, the Doer must discover himself. It is no coincidence that many find their

[14] Georges Gusdorf, *Speaking*, trans. Paul T. Brockelman (Evanston, Ill.: Northwestern University Press, 1965), p. 70.

[15] Jean-Paul Sartre, *Essays in Existentialism* (New York: Citadel Press, 1967), p. 36.

identity in law schools, for an understanding of the law, which binds the citizen and his institutions, is a highly useful civic weapon in calling society to account.[16]

We wouldn't for a moment deny the usefulness of legal training as an instrument of both self-discovery and social change. But it is equally difficult to deny, that while everyone can't attend law school, everyone does need to discover his own identity and his role in relationship to the society in which he lives. We contend, toward this end, not only that ideas in order to be relevant in public speaking must come through self-discovery—but also that such self-discovery is in itself enhanced by a genuine involvement in the act of public speech.

Confronting the ideas necessary to meaningful public speech must inevitably lead to more penetrating thinking about issues of deep concern, as well as compel people who have not thought before to think, to clarify, and to form opinions. In addition, at a more abstract level, the very fact of increased concern for language, which is inherent in thoughtful public speaking, contributes to an expanded awareness and consciousness. As philosopher Georges Gusdorf has put it:

> Speaking constitutes the essence of the world and the essence of man. Each sentence orients us in a world which, moreover, is not given as such, once and for all, but appears to be constructed word by word. Even the most insignificant expression contributes to the work of continuous reconstruction. Just as each word mastered by the young child increases his universe, so too for the adult the act of speaking continually contributes to existence.[17]

The process of discovery and creativity, though accessible to every person, is not an easy one. It would be nice if we could simply will it to happen. As always seems to be the case in such endeavors, however, the inspiration that leads to fulfillment

[16] *Time*, October 18, 1968, p. 47.
[17] Gusdorf, *Speaking*, pp. 37–38.

occurs only after we have invested a lot of hard work. The following scene from Boris Pasternak's *Doctor Zhivago* illustrates the point:

He went back into the warm, well-lit room and began to write. Careful to convey the living movement of his hand in his flowing writing, so that even outwardly it should not lose individuality and grow numb and soulless, he set down, gradually improving them and moving further and further away from the original as he made copy after copy, the poems that he remembered best and that had taken the most definite shape in his mind—"Christmas Star," "Winter Night," and a number of others of the same kind, which later were forgotten, mislaid, and never found again.

From these old, completed poems, he went on to others that he had begun and left unfinished, getting into their spirit and sketching the sequels, though without the slightest hope of finishing them now. Finally getting into his stride and carried away, he started on a new poem.

After two or three stanzas and several images by which he himself was struck, his work took possession of him and he felt the approach of what is called inspiration. At such moments the relation of the forces that determine artistic creation is, as it were, reversed. The dominant thing is no longer the state of mind the artist seeks to express but the language in which he wants to express it. Language, the home and receptacle of beauty and meaning, itself begins to think and speak for man and turns wholly into music, not in terms of sonority but in terms of the impetuousness and power of its inward flow. Then, like the current of a mighty river polishing stones and turning wheels by its very movement, the flow of speech creates in passing, by virtue of its own laws, meter and rhythm and countless other relationships, which are even more important, but which are as yet unexplored, insufficiently recognized, and unnamed.

At such moments Yurii Andreievich felt that the main part of the work was being done not by him but by a superior power which was above his and directed him, namely the movement of universal thought and poetry in its present historical stage and the one to come. And he felt himself to be only the occasion, the fulcrum, needed to make this movement possible.[18]

revealing the self

Hugh Hefner, the successful and articulate publisher of *Playboy* magazine, was once asked in an interview how he came to write the rather lengthy editorial series called the "Playboy Philosophy." Here's what Hefner answered: When the magazine first came out it was criticized by a variety of people for what they assumed it to represent. I just decided that if I was to be damned, I'd rather be damned for what I really believed than for what someone surmised I believed.[19]

The point is worthwhile; people do have a propensity to make judgments about those with whom they come into contact. If they don't have enough information to make a valid judgment, they infer what they need to know and make the judgment anyway. This information concerning human behavior should have special meaning to the public speaker.

people like people

It means, to begin with, that your audience is interested in you as an individual, not as some sort of message-relay machine. The fact that you are the speaker puts you in direct relationship with every individual member of the audience. "People," Brown and Van Riper verify, "are interested in people. They prick up their ears and respond more visibly when they hear egocentric speech. The personal pronouns and statements about self are little gongs that ring for attention and

[18] Boris Pasternak, *Doctor Zhivago* (New York: Pantheon Books, a Division of Random House, Inc., 1958), p. 437.

[19] From a film of the Playboy Club opening in Montreal, Canada, by Playboy Clubs International.

arouse judgmental responses. The personal anecdote always seems to have some special power in this regard."[20]

We have on our campus a student who has become known for his ability to speak effectively on the problems of civil rights. What many of his admirers are not aware of, however, is that this youth's dynamism is in no small measure attributable, not only to his ideas, but to his willingness to "lay it on the line." Both the extent of his self-image and his disposition to reveal himself are suggested in this opening sentence of a speech recently addressed to a student-faculty forum: "I," the speaker began, "am an uppity nigger." Undoubtedly, the abrasiveness of his language had something to do with the attention he received. Consider the difference, however, if he had begun: "I am here to report what some of my 'uppity nigger' friends really think." The shock phrase "uppity nigger" is retained, but the magnetism and intimacy of the original version are almost entirely lost.

If we approach our listeners honestly and openly with the idea, "I want to tell you something that makes a difference to me," they will listen with anticipation for what you are about to reveal concerning your values. If, however, they suspect that you are only parroting an idea copied from someone else, their interest will wane considerably.

to see ourselves as others see us

The propensity of people to judge others on the basis of whatever information and inferences they have available has a second significance to the public speaker. It not only means, as we have just discussed, that your audience is interested in you as an individual, it also means that through the reactions of his listeners the sensitive speaker has a unique opportunity to gain self-insight. If you learn, as all successful speakers do, to

[20] Charles T. Brown and Charles Van Riper, *Speech and Man* (Englewood Cliffs, N.J.: Prentice-Hall, © 1966), p. 48.

read the many cues provided by an audience, you will have an accurate reflection of yourself as others see you.

Such self-insight means everything when dealing with others —whether the relationship is person to person or speaker to audience. In this sense, as an advertisement for the Dale Carnegie Course observes, "There *is* no such thing as 'public' speaking. There is only private speaking—from one mouth to one ear at a time."[21] Not being able to see ourselves as we appear to others will obviously deter any effort to establish productive interpersonal relationships. Each of us can probably recall a number of instances when he has been personally involved in this kind of problem, but it was brought to our attention most recently by someone who told this story:

> Since I'm fairly new to college teaching I guess that I'm probably more concerned than most that my classes be taught with a proper sense of decorum. Still, I do want them to be informal and interesting to the students. Well, I was satisfied that I'd been able to achieve a pretty good balance until the other day when one of my better students came in for an appointment to discuss her term paper. We had, I thought, a cordial conversation, and she thanked me for my help as she got up to leave. Then, almost as she was out the door, she turned and blurted, "I was scared to death to come in to see you, but you've been very nice."
>
> I was shocked, but my curiosity couldn't let the visit end on that kind of note, so I asked her back in to explain why she had been afraid. In the next ten minutes I discovered that the class thought of me as "distant," "cold," "aloof," and "something of a stuffed-shirt." I've never been so surprised in my life! Sure, I'd like to behave with a little dignity—it seems appropriate to the position—but I never meant to give an impression like that.

As complex, many-faceted organisms, each of us has a number of "real" selves. The problem is to determine which of these real selves will affect which people in what way. In

21 *Newsweek*, January 22, 1968, p. 10.

be relevant

public speaking, "we have perhaps the most efficient tool that has been invented for scanning our listeners. By revealing one of our many sides of self and scrutinizing the feedback, we can explore not only our audience but ourselves."[22]

relevance and the other

Throughout our discussion of relevance as it concerns the speaker, we have, you may have noticed, found it necessary to refer to his relationship to others. We now turn to a more detailed consideration of the listener as a factor in the process of being relevant.

meaning is perception

The precept "meaning is perception" is borrowed from a poster one of our graduate school professors had hanging on the wall over his desk. The concept it refers to, though time-honored in the annals of communication theory, has never been better illustrated than in an old Vietnamese folktale.

It seems that a young Buddhist monk who found pleasures of the flesh more to his taste than those of the spirit had begun to neglect the duties of his office. Hearing rumors of his indiscretions, the pagoda's elders decided that their monk's fitness should be tested by a famous holy man whose pilgrimage would soon bring him to their village. Terrified at the prospect of such an examination, the monk exchanged clothes and places with his friend, a cobbler, who for some reason was confident of his ability to pass the test.

Thus, the holy man, though he had taken a vow of silence and communicated only through gestures, appeared at the appointed time and prepared himself for the examination.[23]

---

[22] Brown and Van Riper, *Speech and Man*, p. 48.

[23] From *Playboy* magazine, March 1968; excerpted from "The Boisterous Bonze Thich Xuan," retold by G. W. Victor from a Vietnamese folktale; copyright © 1968 by HMH Publishing Co. Inc.

He then turned to the monk and touched his forehead with the palm of his right hand. The spurious bonze replied by stamping several times with his left foot. The venerable pilgrim smiled and touched his armpit. The young monk immediately patted himself behind. The smile of the examiner grew wider still and he raised the first three fingers of his right hand. His silent companion answered by stretching all five fingers as high and as wide as possible.

The examination was over and the holy man seemed highly satisfied. After saluting the supposed monk respectfully, he rejoined the notables waiting in a group outside the pagoda and asked for a brush and paper. He wrote: "I have visited many pagodas between here and Siam, but never did I meet a monk as learned in the doctrine as your bonze. He not only answered my questions perfectly but he responded with the subtle parables that show great learning. I said to him: 'We must always cherish the Buddha image in our head.' And he replied: 'We must fiercely stamp out the illusions of Mara the Tempter.' Then I showed my armpit to indicate: 'The prayers of the just mount to heaven as if tucked by the stork under his delicate wings.' He replied: 'The stork disappears in the clouds, but the dependable tortoise stays on to carry the heavy stele of remembrance on his rounded back.' Then I quoted the phrase: 'The three stars of the faith shine under the celestial arch.' And immediately he replied: 'The five joys enter the home of the faithful.' These citations are all taken from the holy writings and they form parables worthy of a great master. Your young bonze has gone far in the ways of faith. I congratulate you on your choice."

With the holy man's report concluded, the elders made their way to the pagoda, prostrated themselves before the monk, and begged his forgiveness.

No sooner had they gone than the two friends embraced and congratulated each other. "But what in the world did you do?" asked the bonze.

"Your holy man is nothing but a fraud," replied the cobbler. "As soon as he saw me, he asked if I was a hatmaker. I stamped my foot on the ground to show that I make shoes.

be relevant

45

Then he pointed to his armpits to let me know he wanted a pair of sandals cut from the supple flank of the beast. I showed him my back to explain that the leather from that part is tougher and better adapted to the dusty trails of a pilgrimage. He offered me three piasters for a pair. But I asked for five and he left. Perhaps he found my price too high."

For most of us, as this story so well illustrates, *our* world is *the* world. It is difficult for us to imagine that everyone does not see the world just as we do. Furthermore, this is as true of our perception of words as it was of the cobbler's and holy man's perceptions of gestures. We tend to operate on the basis of what Irving Lee has called "the purist's dogma."[24] That is, we behave in communication situations as though words had some definite, accurate meaning of their own, regardless of the person using them. This, of course, is not true. Meanings are in people, not in words, and people, as in the case of our Vietnamese folktale, differ markedly.

a rose is [not necessarily] a rose

When we talk about meaning in communication we are referring to something that goes far beyond, for example, the ability of different persons to apply the same label or name to an item when it is shown to them. If, for illustration, we were to hold up a familiarly shaped bottle with a label depicting four roses on the front, chances are that we would not have too much difficulty getting most adults to accept the word "whiskey" as an appropriate name. Once we have done this, however, we have still come nowhere near to understanding the *meaning* that this item has for those agreeing to the label "whiskey." The following excerpt from a speech by T. F. Patton makes the point.

Mr. Patton is telling a story about a young lawyer who was

[24] Irving J. Lee, *How to Talk with People* (New York: Harper & Row, 1952), p. 22.

running for the state legislature in Mississippi. The lawyer had been asked by a leading newspaper about the controversial wet-dry issue facing the state. Here is his reply, as Patton recounted it:

Dear Sir:

I had not intended to discuss this controversial subject at this particular time. However, I want you to know that I do not shun a controversy. On the contrary, I'll take a stand on any issue at any time, regardless of how fraught with controversy it may be. You have asked me how I feel about whiskey. Well, here's how I stand on the question. If, when you say whiskey, you mean the Devil's Brew, the Poison Scourge, the Bloody Monster that defies innocence, dethrones reason, creates misery and poverty, yea literally takes the bread out of the mouths of babes; if you mean the evil drink that topples the Christian man and woman from pinnacles of righteous, gracious living into the bottomless pit of despair, degradation, shame, helplessness and hopelessness, then . . . I am against it with all my power.

But, if, when you say whiskey, you mean the oil of conversation, the philosophic wine and ale that is consumed when good fellows get together, that puts a song in their hearts, laughter on their lips and the warm glow of contentment in their eyes; if you mean Christmas cheer, if you mean the stimulating drink that puts the spring in an old man's step on a frosty morning; . . . if you mean that drink, the sale of which pours into our treasury untold millions of dollars, which are used to provide tender care for our little crippled children, our blind, our deaf, our dumb, our pitifully aged and infirm, and to build highways, hospitals, and schools, then . . . I am for it.

This is my stand; I will not retract from it. I will not compromise.[25]

That those with whom he wants to communicate may see and value things in ways different than he does is an axiom

---

[25] T. F. Patton, "Manpower Development in a Changing World," *Vital Speeches of the Day*, Vol. 31 (November 15, 1964), p. 88. Reprinted by special permission.

that the speaker must not forget if he is to be effective. In practical terms, it means that as public speakers we must be willing and able to adjust our messages to our audiences.

Audience adjustment or adaptation has sometimes been misinterpreted as dishonesty or insincerity. But this is not the case at all. What it means is that the speaker is knowledgeable in his use of language. He realizes that the important thing in communication is not the words themselves, but the meaning they communicate. If the speaker wishes to communicate a certain idea, he will need to discover those words and expressions that will convey the intended idea to the audience. It matters not at all that these may not be the same words or expressions he would personally prefer.

To make the kind of audience adaptation necessary to the successful communication of meaning implies that a speaker must study and understand his audience. This goes well beyond the conventional idea of accumulating information about his listeners such as their ages, sex, religion, occupation, and politics. It is not the information as such but the use it is put to that makes the difference. Essentially, successful audience adaptation requires that the speaker become what is often called a student of human nature.

It is, admittedly, much easier to declare that we must all become students of human nature than it is to accomplish the necessary insights. Awareness of the problem and practice in speaking in public will, however, do much to sharpen our sensitivity to the feelings of others.

The first step, we feel, is to develop an awareness of the problem. And that's what we've been attempting to accomplish in this discussion of "relevance and the other." People *do* see things differently; they *do* assign different values; words *don't* mean the same thing to all people; *our* world is *not* the same as *the* world. Telling it "like it is," we must understand, is a matter of meaning and value. Our job as speakers is to determine those words that for our audience will communicate the meanings and values we wish to convey.

Ralph Nader is a young lawyer who has become famous during the mid-1960s for his single-handed attacks on the giants of American industry. In 1966, while testifying before a United States Senate subcommittee hearing concerning the safety standards of Detroit's auto makers, Nader was asked why he was doing all this. Here is his answer: "I became in a sense incensed at the way there can be a tremendous amount of injustice and brutality in an industrialized society, without any responsibility. This is a problem of individuals confronting complex organizations. It is not an equal contest."[26]

It may not be an equal contest, but Ralph Nader and many others like him have demonstrated that individuals need not be powerless. Commenting on this issue in an essay, the editors of *Time* magazine wrote: "To the angry, the answer lately has been protest, demonstration, riot. And violence does bring a sense of power, does achieve change—though more often it brings only violent reaction. There are other ways, and they work."[27]

Examples of these "other ways" and how they work are at every hand once one starts to look for them.[28]

When a Roman Catholic gynecologist, Dr. John Rock, signed his name to a birth-control petition nearly forty years ago there appeared little chance that his church's hierarchy would ever change its position on this issue. Working over the years, both as a scientist helping to develop the birth-control pill and as a persuader enlisting others to his belief, Dr. Rock has been influential in altering the attitudes and practices of Catholics and non-Catholics alike.

[26] *Time,* October 18, 1968, p. 46.

[27] *Time,* October 18, 1968, p. 46.

[28] Information for these examples taken from *Time,* October 18, 1968, pp. 46–47.

Two years ago James Lorenz, a young lawyer then in his twenties, gave up his private law practice in order to help his state's agricultural workers, many of them itinerant laborers. His goal was to provide these people with protection from gyp-merchants and others who attempt to exploit their lack of education. In the process, Lorenz's organization, California Rural Legal Assistance, Inc., took more than 4,000 cases to court and won more than 85 percent of them.

Lou Smith, a young, black militant, demonstrated that one need not be a doctor or lawyer in order to have an impact on society. Smith, who discarded revolution as impractical, said, "There are greater forces than violence and confrontation." Through conviction and persuasion, he induced others to join with him in forming Operation Bootstrap. Through self-help and without any government aid, the organization established a number of black-owned and black-operated businesses, as well as a school for the purpose of developing pride, black culture, and job training. Smith stated his belief: "Change is going to come in this country, and it's going to come from the bottom to the top."

In each of these cases, and in thousands like them, "ordinary" people have shown an awareness of what Otis Walter and Robert Scott refer to as "the circle of influence."[29] Each of us, like the pebble dropped into a pond, can initiate ripples that extend well beyond our immediate vicinity. "In a mass society," the editors of one news magazine note, "everything is so interrelated that small actions may have big effects, all of them widely reported by mass communications. In short, today's individual is anything but powerless against The System. He can easily disrupt it—for good or evil."[30]

For you, the readers of this book, these ideas should have special significance. Every time you get a chance to speak, you are in a position to exert influence—to exercise power. This

[29] Otis M. Walter and Robert L. Scott, *Thinking and Speaking* (New York: Macmillan Co., 1962), p. 7.

[30] *Time*, October 18, 1968, p. 46.

means that in a very real sense there is no such thing as a practice speech since there are no practice audiences. Each group we speak to—class, club, business, social—is composed of real people with real motives who interact both among themselves and with others in other groups. "In these groups," as Walter and Scott emphasize, "we shall inevitably come to grips in some way with the issues that face our times. In these circles we may be influential, and no matter how small the circle or how limited our influence, it is important."[31]

What we've tried to say in this chapter has been well summarized by Maine's Senator Edmund Muskie. Speaking of his experiences during his campaign for the Vice-Presidency, Muskie reported:

> If I learned anything in the campaign, it was that simple communication is a great deal of what the young people of America want. The young understand that being listened to—I mean real listening—is a part of power.
>
> Every citizen can't be President, but every citizen can influence. If he can talk, if he can articulate, if he can persuade, if he can convince . . .[32]

[31] Walter and Scott, *Thinking and Speaking*, p. 7.
[32] *The Kansas City Times*, January 17, 1969, p. 2.

3

be clear

A plumber with a limited command of English discovered that hydrochloric acid opened clogged drains quickly and effectively, but he thought that he had better check with the Bureau of Standards in Washington, D.C., to find out if it was all right to use it. So he wrote a letter to them. A Bureau scientist answered: "The efficacy of hydrochloric acid is indisputable, but the corrosive residue is incompatible with metallic permanence."

The plumber promptly replied, thanking the Bureau scientist for informing him that it was all right to use hydrochloric acid.

This worried the scientist and he showed the letter to his boss. The boss wrote a second letter to the plumber, saying: "We cannot assume responsibility for the production of toxic and noxious residue with hydrochloric acid and suggest that you use an alternative procedure."

By this time, the plumber figured that somebody in Washington really liked him, so he wrote back again thanking them and said that the acid was still working just dandy.

This last letter was passed on to the boss's boss, who broke off the correspondence with a terse note: "Don't use hydrochloric acid. It eats hell out of the pipes."

A communicator needs to make ideas clear in terms of the people he is addressing. When the Bureau scientist wrote, "The efficacy of hydrochloric acid is indisputable, but the corrosive residue is incompatible with permanence," he doubtlessly felt that he had made it quite plain that hydrochloric acid should not be used for opening clogged pipes. Nevertheless, the receiver of his message, the plumber, interpreted it as approval of what he was doing, the exact opposite of the sender's intent. The breakdown in communication obviously resulted from the use of language not relevant to the educational level of the plumber. Being relevant to the listener and selecting language meaningful to him are the first steps toward achieving understanding. But the art of being clear also involves ordering ideas clearly, developing them clearly, and presenting them clearly. As often as not, breakdowns in communication are simply the result of poor organization, inadequate illustration, a failure to explain and define, or, perhaps, even mumbling on the part of the speaker.

focus upon a specific theme

A disconsolate-looking farmer stood on the steps of the town hall during the progress of a political speech. "Do you know who's talking in there now?" demanded a stranger briskly, pausing for a moment beside the farmer. "Or are you just going in?"

"No, sir; I've just come out," said the farmer decidedly. "Congressman Sniffkins is talking in there."

"What about?" asked the stranger.

"Well," continued the farmer, somewhat puzzled, as he rubbed his forehead with his hand, "he didn't say."

The speaker's first tasks in being clear to an audience are to narrow the focus of his subject so that he can treat it meaningfully in the allotted time, to limit himself to one major idea, and to tell the audience quite specifically the basic message of his speech. Beginning speakers frequently fail in their quest to be clear and meaningful simply because they treat their subject too generally and use more than one major idea. A student in one of our classes once gave a five-minute speech on the economic and military problems of World War II. Considering himself a good student and a better-than-average speaker, he was quite surprised to receive a low grade. He felt that he had chosen a large, worthwhile subject with multiple facets and had discussed it well. That's just it. He had chosen a "large" subject and a "multiple" subject for a five-minute speech! To be sure, his subject was worthwhile, but his discussion of it had to be imprecise and superficial.

The surest means of getting one's theme, or main idea, across to people is to tell them explicitly what it is, not once, but several times during the speech. The introduction of the speech may be used to disclose and clarify the speaker's central thought. Observe how speech student Tim Kelley did this in a speech on Indian education.

A nineteen-year-old Navajo Indian in a two-room dwelling with a dirt floor sits down to his meal of coffee and bread. He is tired from the day's work of hauling water five miles and chopping wood for heat. Later, as he prepares for bed, he says goodnight to his parents in Navajo for he knows little of the white man's language. This Indian is not from the nineteenth century. He is the Indian today.

When we enjoy the latest John Wayne western on television, do we think of the Indian today whose life expectancy is only 42 years? On some reservations a child has little chance of escaping his fate. A baby born on the Papago reservation in southwestern Arizona may expect to live only 17 years, while the average life of a white person in the United States is now 68 and that of a Negro is 60. According to a recent United States congressional appraisal of the American Indian situation, the Indians have the highest birth rate and the highest death rate; their unemployment rates are the highest; they have a growing population with a steadily decreasing and already inadequate land base; they have the least political power and lowest standard of living; and they have the lowest educational level of achievement and the highest illiteracy rate of any group of Americans.

What can be done to bring the Indians into the prosperity we enjoy? What can be done to help the American Indians begin to help themselves? Education is one answer. Education can create strength among the 600,000 Indians of America. But this problem cannot be solved by more education alone; it must also be the right type of education.

be clear

Tim Kelley was not content merely to state his subject at the end of his introduction and let it go at that; rather he used repeated thematic emphasis to assure clarity. The following statements, taken from Tim Kelley's speech, illustrate how he focused upon his central thought at appropriate intervals throughout his speech. "What is the right type of education for the Indian?" "Would that be the right type of education?" "Education is the Indian's hope, but the wrong type of education can be a shattering experience." "We must not only educate, but we must educate in the right way." "The quality and amount of Indian education must be raised. But we must also educate with vision and imagination. The right type of education is needed."

In conclusion, Tim Kelley focused sharply upon his central theme one final time.

> You and I know the importance of an education, for we realize it as we experience each new class in school. Let us not deny the Indian boys and girls and men and women the chance to experience and learn as much as we do. Let us not allow the Indians, our fellow Americans, to remain weak from being ignorant and illiterate. Let us not continue to provide the Indians, the original Americans, with a one-sided education that they only reject. Rather let us provide the Indian with more of the right type of education.

use only a few main points

The average speech listener probably feels like President Lincoln when he became annoyed with the complicated red tape reports, containing many points, that came to his desk in the White House. He objected to them with a typical Lincoln aphorism: "When I send a man to buy a horse, I don't want to be told how many hairs the horse has in his tail. I wish only to know his main points."

The central idea of a speech is developed through a series of subordinate statements that constitute the "main points" of the message. These main points tell essentially what a speaker thinks or believes about his subject. A speech, in a sense, is an analysis of a given subject, and when one analyzes something one breaks it down into its essential components in order to inspect it more closely. A large number of developmental points make a speech confusing and hard to remember. More than five in any speech may well be excessive. From two to four is usually best.

Billy Graham, the prominent evangelist, probably speaks to more people each year than any other living American. Millions hear him on the radio or see him on television. Thousands flock to hear him speak in person during a crusade. Billy Graham is a successful evangelist for more reasons than one, but an important factor in his success is his rhetorical skill. His addresses are always easy to follow, which is attributable to clear thinking and the use of only a few, clearly stated main points. In a sermon on "Pride" he used the following main points, carefully partitioning and forecasting them in his introduction—which reads in part:

> Pride may take various forms, but it all emanates from the haughty human heart. Some take pride in their looks, others in their race, others in their business, others in their social life. In other words, pride may be spiritual, intellectual, material or social.[1]

Graham then uses the following statements as lead-ins to the four main points of his speech as he gets to them: "The most repugnant of these four is spiritual pride." "Another form of pride is intellectual pride." "Still another manifestation of pride is the pride of material things." "Then there is social pride."

[1] Billy Graham, *Seven Deadly Sins* (Minneapolis, Minn.: The Billy Graham Evangelistic Association, 1955), pp. 7–8.

be clear

Suppose you take a deck of cards and toss them aimlessly on the floor, with most of the cards falling in their usual random manner. Accidentally, however, some of the cards fall so as to draw a rough configuration of a star. As you look at the cards on the floor, what attracts your attention? Almost certainly those cards that form a shape that you can recognize —the star. Let's further suppose that all four queens happened to fall so that they form a small cluster of cards apart from the others. These queens also will attract your attention. To carry this idea further, look up at the stars at night. What attracts your attention? The brightest stars—and what else? Those that have recognizable form, such as the Big Dipper. The lesson is simple. People are always looking for recognizable forms. The Rorschach Inkblot Test is based on this principle. Part of the pleasure of putting together a jigsaw puzzle is to watch the form of the puzzle develop. It stands to reason also that members of a listening audience like to be able to recognize the form of a speech and to observe the unfolding of its design.

This is not to say that relatively formless, or perhaps even totally formless, speeches cannot be effective. Sometimes the orator's personal magnetism and the emotional sweep of his address are such that an audience will be enthralled by a speech that really is quite amorphous. One noted critic of contemporary discourse has quite properly observed that much of today's talk is lacking in classical modes of arrangement; in its place we have formlessness or stream-of-consciousness patterns.

Gone from such contemporary discourse are the familiar introduction, body, and conclusion; the statement and partition of issues; internal summaries; topical, spatial, chronological or any other particular kind of order. More typically today the spokesmen for peace or war in Vietnam, bussing or non-bussing of school children, legalizing or cracking down on marijuana, or the pros and cons of the cohabitation of college coeds, begin to talk with rambling personal experiences, sometimes rather dramatic, and finish about where they started, with a liberal sprinkling of "you knows" in between.[2]

Nevertheless, for most speeches, at least if clarity is an objective, a definiteness of order is useful. Despite the current practices of certain contemporary speakers, most audiences, if given the choice, would prefer to have a clearly structured and well-designed presentation. Not only is listening made easier but also they find a certain comfort and security in being able to recognize a familiar form. Probably the less trouble the audience has in following the speaker the greater the chances of his getting his message across. A careful and strategic ordering of ideas will help the thought of the speech to progress logically from one point to another.

Certain subjects quite naturally divide themselves into topics or main points. If so, these divisions usually can be used with profit. Billy Graham's sermon on "Pride," for example, employs the natural partitioning of "spiritual, intellectual, material, and social." Some other natural categories are: political, economic, and social; local, state, and national; past, present, and future; problem, causes, and solution; background, characteristics, and accomplishments; resemblances and differences; specific to general; general to specific; theory and practice; East to West; and a classification of types—such as hunting dogs, watch dogs, and show dogs. Many more can be cited.

Of course, not all speech subjects can be divided so neatly. If, for example, one cites three reasons why ROTC programs should be banned from college campuses, he will have to decide what is the best way of ordering his reasons in terms of the most logical unfolding of his subject for the audience he is addressing.

[2] Franklyn S. Haiman, "The Rhetoric of 1968: A Farewell to Rational Discourse," in *The Ethics of Controversy: Politics and Protest*, Proceedings of the First Annual Symposium on Issues in Public Communication, eds. Donn W. Parson and Wil A. Linkugel (Lawrence: University of Kansas, 1968), pp. 126–127.

Meaningful thought bridges between main points give the speech coherence. They provide signposts as to where the speaker is in his speech, where he has been, and where he is going. Sometimes it is useful to number points and explicitly tell the audience that one is moving from his "second" to his "third" point. Moreover, an occasional summary, which tells what one has covered and relates what will follow, will help to make the flow of ideas clear. As a minimum, transitions should end and round off the preceding point and clearly direct the listener to the next point of development. Student speakers have used the following three transitions in their speeches:

> Having defined what I mean by "sensationalism," let's examine how it differs from yellow journalism.

> The two primary causes of water pollution, thus, are that cities use rivers as sewers and factories dump their wastes in them. Having thus established that our nation's waterways are becoming polluted and why this is happening, let's take a look at some possible solutions to the problem.

> The first characteristic of a good teacher, thus, is imaginativeness. The second is patience.

illustrate, compare, and contrast

In the late 1940s, Rudolf Flesch published two books, *The Art of Plain Talk* (1946) and *The Art of Readable Writing* (1949). In these books Dr. Flesch was concerned with clarity in communication. He advocated "up-and-down" writing so that a speech or a composition consists of a series of "peaks and valleys," the peaks being the abstract thought and the valleys the concrete cases, illustrations, and examples. We feel that his statement contains some of the best advice for making ideas clear that we have encountered: "As a rule, you should never stay at the abstract level for long; as soon as you get there, turn around and plunge again into the down-to-earth world of people and things. This 'up-and-down' writing is the only protection against misunderstanding."[3] A dull and difficult-to-understand speech invariably consists of too much abstract thought and not enough clarifying and illustrative material. To be clear, all abstract general statements can profitably be followed with a "downward" movement to the concrete and illustrative level.

An excellent example of Dr. Flesch's "up-and-down" theory of speaking is a speech by Dr. Karl Menninger, the world-renowned psychiatrist. Mental illness is a subject that a psychiatrist could discuss in such an abstract manner that a lay audience would understand very little. Dr. Menninger's speech, "Healthier than Healthy," however, is crystal clear. Note his "up-and-down" style in the following section from his address:[4]

The fourth observation I wanted to make is that some patients may have a mental illness and then get well, and then may even get "weller"! I mean they get better than they ever were. They get even better than they were before. This is an extraordinary and little-realized truth—and it constitutes the main point of my talk today.

After making the above general statement, and then restating it, down he goes to a concrete example:

Abraham Lincoln was undoubtedly a far more productive, a far bigger man, and a far broader and wiser man after his

[3] Rudolf Flesch, *The Art of Readable Writing* (New York: Harper & Row, 1949), pp. 164–165.

[4] From "Healthier than Healthy," a speech by Karl Menninger, M.D., reprinted in full in *Contemporary American Speeches*, 2nd ed., eds. Wil A. Linkugel, R. R. Allen, and Richard L. Johannesen (Belmont, Calif.: Wadsworth Publishing Co., 1969), pp. 54–63. The text of this speech is from *A Psychiatrist's World*, by Karl Menninger, M.D. Copyright © 1959 by Karl Menninger, M.D. Reprinted by permission of The Viking Press, Inc.

attack of mental illness than he was before. Prior to it he seemed to fail at everything—in his profession, in politics, in love. After this terrible year of depression, he rose to the great heights of vision and accomplishment for which we all know him. And Lincoln is not the only one; there are many others, but he is a conspicuous one.

Menninger follows the Lincoln example with a general statement phrased in the form of a question: "Now I ask you, does this occur in physical illness?" Right back down he goes to a comparison of two concrete examples:

It was noticed in England by a very observing doctor, Dr. Jenner, that some of the milkmaids caught a disease called "cowpox." They subsequently seemed to be a little healthier in some respects than did the other people. Particularly when smallpox came, which was one of the great plagues of the world, as you know, it was noticed that these milkmaids didn't get it. From that it was gradually discovered through a process of some numerous steps that if you get cowpox, you are in some way or other protected against getting smallpox. Now this idea of inoculation, giving you one disease to prevent your getting another, is a kind of a way of making you "weller" than you were before, in that you are protected against something that you previously haven't been protected against. Cowpox being less serious than smallpox, most of us are glad to have it. Of course most of us have had it now. Cowpox got to be one of the great popular diseases of the world and everybody tried to get it, just as we try to have our little girls and boys get the German measles to protect them against serious trouble later.

Dr. Menninger follows this comparison with two additional illustrations, then moves back to the more abstract level and makes explicit the point he is trying to make:

The point that I am trying to develop is the old principle that sometimes one illness can, in some way or other, drive out another illness.

a time to speak

62

After reading the above section from Dr. Menninger's speech, it is not hard to understand why he held the interest of his audience and why they understood exactly what he was trying to say. He brought his ideas down to the concrete level of people and experiences through illustration, comparison, and contrast.

Historically, some of the most successful speeches have been filled with illustrative materials. The most listened-to speech of the nineteenth century and the early part of the twentieth century, Russell Conwell's "Acres of Diamonds," which will be referred to more extensively in Chapter 5, consists of about 75 percent illustration of the idea that wealth and abundance are found not in distant lands but in one's own back yard. The use of illustrations was the most distinctive single feature of the preaching of Henry Ward Beecher, the most renowned clergyman of the nineteenth century whose Brooklyn church was packed virtually every Sunday with more than two thousand people. He discussed illustrations in his *Yale Lectures on Preaching:*

> Illustrations are as natural to me as breathing; I use fifty now to one in the early years of my ministry. . . . Experience has taught that not only are persons pleased by being instructed through illustration, but they are more readily instructed thus, because, substantially, the mode in which we learn a new thing is by its being likened to something which we already know. They are a kind of covert analogy, or likening one thing to another, so that obscure things become plain, being represented pictorially or otherwise by things that are not obscure and that we are familiar with.[5]

[5] Henry Ward Beecher, *Yale Lectures on Preaching*, 1st Series (New York: J. B. Ford and Co., 1873), p. 155.

The following passage on crime in America illustrates what's wrong with much of our speaking:

> Crime in this country is on a runaway course. For the past several decades it has been on the increase. Frequency of violence has probably increased several times since the turn of the century or thereabouts. Within recent years, this increase in crime has continued. You may even have some close friends who have been affected by this growing problem. Something must be done.

Such talk is vague, unclear, and hopelessly dull. Only a cursory analysis of the statement is necessary to determine the problem and its remedy: it needs to be made specific and concrete.

> The crime rate has increased steadily in America during the twentieth century until it is now the most critical and urgent domestic problem facing the nation. From 1940, just prior to World War II, to 1964, aggravated assaults increased 48 percent, forcible rape 5 percent and robberies over 12 percent. From 1960 to 1968, there has been an increase in crime of 88 percent, while the population of the nation has increased only 10 percent. One third of a representative sample of all Americans say it is unsafe to walk alone at night in their neighborhoods and more than one third say they keep firearms in the house for protection. Last night's newspaper listed three murders, eleven robberies, and seven cases of assault. You may even have close friends who have been victims of such crimes. I have. My older brother was an innocent bystander who was struck by a bullet during a robbery. It was then that I decided something had to be done to deter crime in our cities.

We recall two orations a few years ago on the general subject of nuclear weapons control. The two speeches contained passages that offered striking contrasts. The first speaker never left the level of the general idea:

Stop and think about this problem tonight. And if you do you will realize that if irresponsible enemy forces have access to uncontrolled nuclear weapons they may destroy our land, our city, and perhaps even our homes.

The second speaker said:

When you go home tonight, look at the grass and trees in your yard, look at your home. Observe the happiness and joy on the faces of the neighbor kids as they are playing ball in the street. Listen to your children shriek with glee as they see you coming up the sidewalk. Then think. Think of an irresponsible enemy with the power to scorch every blade of grass, to conflagrate every board of your home, and destroy your loved ones and the neighbor kids playing ball in the street. Multiply and spread this effect throughout your city, indeed throughout the country, and you have a good picture of the awesome devastation that may come from a nuclear holocaust.

use special emphasis devices

A speech scholar named Ray Ehrensberger researched the problem of giving emphasis to important points.[6] The results were startling. He found, for example, if you want to be sure that your listeners get some information of critical importance, you will do well to tell them, "Now get this . . ." In Ehrensberger's experiment, 86 percent of the listeners got the information when it was preceded by a statement such as, "Now get this"; whereas only 53.2 percent got it when no emphasis device was used. This was found to be a statistically significant difference at the highest level of confidence. In line with this principle, the authors have observed that, whenever they inform their students during a lecture that a certain piece

[6] Ray Ehrensberger, "An Experimental Study of the Relative Effectiveness of Certain Forms of Emphasis in Public Speaking," *Speech Monographs*, Vol. 12 (1945), pp. 94–111.

of information will probably be on the next examination, students suddenly start reaching for their pencils and notebooks to write it down. In writing, we underscore or italicize statements of unusual importance. A verbal underscoring of such statements with a "Now get this," "This is especially important," or "Be sure not to miss this" will help you to get vital ideas across to your listeners.

define and explain

Too often people fail to understand each other simply because they do not define what they mean by the words they use. In private conversation we often pause in our discussion to ask, "What do you mean by that?" The members of a large audience, conforming to cultural norms, almost never do that. It is thus critical for the speaker himself to be alert for words and concepts that need explanation. New and unusual words, very abstract words, and jargon—if unfamiliar to the audience —need definition. Frequently, an elementary dictionary definition will suffice; often simple rephrasing or the citation of a synonym or antonym will make meaning clear. Sometimes an example is needed to assure accuracy of meaning. Note how Stokely Carmichael, the Black Power orator, successfully deals with the word "syllogism" in talking to a black audience:

> There's a thing called a syllogism. And it says like, if you're born in Detroit, you're beautiful; that's the major premise. The minor premise is—I am born in Detroit. Therefore, I am beautiful. Anything all black is bad—major premise. Minor premise—I am all black. Therefore [pause], yeah, yeah [laughter and applause] yeah. You're all out there, and the man telling you that anything all black is bad, and you talking about yourself, and you don't even know it.[7]

[7] "Stokely Carmichael Explains Black Power to a Black Audience in Detroit," in *The Rhetoric of Black Power*, eds. Robert L. Scott and Wayne Brockriede (New York: Harper & Row, 1969), p. 88.

A good rule is to keep jargon at a minimum. Jargon may impress some people, but it is almost sure to confuse a lot more. Athletics, the military, and the social sciences are specially noted for jargon. The use of it may be very meaningful when speaking to someone of the same field; but, whenever an attempt is made to communicate with someone outside the fraternity, the most common words appropriate should be used. A social scientist demonstrated this problem in writing about the *social component:*

> [It] includes the potentialities for social relations as they are affected by "the number of human beings in the situation, their distribution in space, their ages, their sex, their native ability to interstimulate and interact, the interference of environmental hindrances or helps, and the presence and amount of certain types of social equipment."[8]

We are willing to bet that as you read the quotation you had no idea the author was speaking of courtship!

It is of interest that Dr. Karl Menninger, from whom we quoted earlier, uses the language of his trade well, but when he presented "Healthier than Healthy" to a lay audience at Chautauqua, New York, he used everyday language.

Richard Weaver, in a stimulating book titled *The Ethics of Rhetoric*, devotes one chapter to "The Rhetoric of Social Science." Weaver points out that we use two kinds of terms in our speech—"positive" and "dialectical"—and it is eminently clear that positive terms are concrete and dialectical terms are abstract.

> The positive term designates something existing simply in the objective world: the chair, the tree, the farm. Arguments over positive terms are not arguments in the true sense, since the point at issue is capable of immediate and public settlement, just as one might settle an "argument" over the width of a room by bringing in a publicly-agreed-upon yardstick.

[8] Donald L. Taylor, "Courtship as a Social Institution in the United States, 1930–1945," *Social Forces*, Vol. 25 (October 1946), p. 68.

Consequently a rhetoric of positive terms is a rhetoric of simple description, which requires only powers of accurate observation and reporting.

It is otherwise with dialectical terms. These are terms standing for concepts, which are defined by their negatives or their privations. "Justice" is a dialectical term which is defined by "injustice"; "social improvement" is made meaningful by the use of "privation of social improvement." To say that a family has an income of $800 a year is positive; to say that the same family is underprivileged is dialectical. It can be underprivileged only with reference to families which have more privileges.[9]

To be sure, dialectical terms are necessary to the communication of ideas. But it is equally sure that positive expressions are infinitely clearer. When abstract, dialectical terms are used, definition and explanation are essential for clarity.

use extraverbal aids

When you impart information to a group of listeners by talking to them, how much of the information do you think they will retain three days later? 75 percent? 50 percent? 25 percent? None of these guesses is correct. The fact is that they will remember only 10 percent! Most of us think that this is an unsatisfactory amount. But can it be improved? It can. Robert S. Craig reported to the 1967 National Osteopathic Child Health Conference that studies conducted at Atlanta show that when knowledge was imparted to a person by telling alone, the recall three hours later was 70 percent, and three days later, only 10 percent. When imparted by showing alone, the knowledge recall three hours later was 72 percent, and three days later, about 35 percent. A marked improvement. But does this mean that we should stop speaking and just show

[9] Richard M. Weaver, *The Ethics of Rhetoric* (Chicago: Henry Regnery, 1953), pp. 187–188.

pictures? Obviously not. "When both telling and showing were the teaching tools," Craig reported, "the recall three hours later was 85 percent, and three days later, 65 percent. This should emphasize that recall increases markedly by using both speech and pictures."[10]

People absorb ideas through sensory perceptions. Telling alone involves only the sense of hearing, but telling and showing involve two senses—hearing and seeing. The more senses one can involve in imparting ideas the greater the degree of comprehension. Take, for example, the case of a person trying to tell someone else about pipe tobacco. Let us assume that the listener has never heard of pipe tobacco, seen pipe tobacco, smelled pipe tobacco, or smoked it. The speaker may begin by telling his listener about pipe tobacco, describing what it looks like, what it smells like, and what it tastes like when smoked in a pipe. But does his listener now really know what pipe tobacco is like? It will help if the speaker brings some pipe tobacco and lets his listener look at it. He will now understand about the color of pipe tobacco and the general size and shape of it. But if the speaker goes one step further and lets his listener pick up some of the pipe tobacco with his fingers he will understand it even better. He can achieve even greater understanding if he allows the listener to smell the tobacco, both in the pouch and as it is being smoked. Now is this total comprehension? We think not. The listener has experienced pipe tobacco through his sense of hearing, seeing, touching, and smelling. But he has not yet tasted it. If he wishes to obtain maximum understanding of pipe tobacco, he needs to smoke some of it and thereby taste it. The point is, the more of the listener's senses the communicator can involve the greater the comprehension of his message.

The primary form of extraverbal aids in speech communication is visual: graphs, charts, pictures, slides, and motion pictures. Objects, such as the display of actual samples in a speech on a new kind of fountain pen, are most helpful. The

[10] Conwell Carson, "Best Memory by Eye and the Ear," *The Kansas City Times*, April 19, 1967, p. 13A.

be clear

chalk board is an ever ready form of visual aid also. Regardless of the visual aid you use, it should be large enough for all to see and should be displayed in such a manner that all can actually see it. It is most frustrating for a listener not to be able to see something that the speaker especially wants him to see. A second guideline for the use of visual aids is to preserve as much eye contact with the audience as one can when using the visuals. When the speaker is finished with the ideas related to them, he will do well to remove the visual aids from sight so they do not become silent competitors for his listeners' attention. As a rule, it is well to avoid passing objects among the audience during a speech. One will lose a lot of attention if members of the audience inspect an object and pass it on to their neighbors while he is speaking.

Although visual aids are the most common, good speakers search for other forms of sensory aids as well. Audio aids can frequently be employed as can the sense of touch when discussing specific objects. Time spent in gathering and preparing extraverbal aids is time well spent; 65 percent recall of information after a three-day period is six and one half times as great as 10 percent.

don't be a mush-mouth

A first class electrician's mate aboard the submarine *Stickleback* stood at the controls and told another electrician's mate to "come off" on his panel. But he failed to speak distinctly, and the second electrician's mate thought he heard him say "come on," and he turned the rheostat the wrong way. The error tripped circuit breakers and cut off the ship's main power. The submarine went out of control and surfaced directly in front of the destroyer escort *Silverstein*. The *Stickleback* was rammed and sunk—because an electrician's mate had failed to enunciate the "f" sound clearly.

The first principle of speech communication is to be heard;

the second is to articulate and enunciate clearly. The most common failing of beginning speakers is that they do not project their voices to the entire audience. It is ironic that people should show so little concern for "being heard" when it is so critical to the communication process. Why bother to speak at all if you're not going to speak loud enough for people to hear you? A good speaker addresses the people in the back row as well as those sitting in front.

Mumbling, faulty articulation of vowel sounds and poor enunciation of consonants make much speaking that we are forced to listen to unintelligible. Indistinct speech may not often be the cause of the destruction of a submarine, but it will be unclear to the listeners—to say nothing of the pain of their having to listen to such mumblings. Listeners tend to tune out on the mumbler and thereby cut off the communication channel.

let your body talk also

Try this experiment with one of your friends. Turn out all the lights in a room at night and pull the shades to make the room as dark as possible. Then try to explain to him proper technique for swinging a golf club. You will be sure to experience frustration because he can only hear you but cannot see your accompanying bodily action. It is then that you will realize the importance of talking with your body also. You will probably need at least twice the number of words to make your ideas clear to your friend as you would if he could see your bodily language in addition to hearing your vocal descriptions. Indeed, your friend could probably grasp the technique you are trying to explain a lot quicker and better if you turned on the light and only used bodily language and spoke no words at all.

Just how instrumental visual signals can be to the communication process is illustrated by the Zuñi Indians. As early as

1909, W. I. Thomas reported that visual signs are so essential to their communication system that it is impossible for them to communicate in the dark. Certain facial and bodily gesticulations are needed for them to make their language intelligible.

The face and body will communicate whether we want them to or not. A person's posture and his general bodily movements (or lack of them), for example, will tell the listener a good deal about his attitudes. It is critical therefore that one's visual cues communicate thoughts consonant to his general purpose. Just how vital a role the visual aspects of the speaker play in communicating attitudes is illustrated by an incident involving Jerry Lewis. Hosting the *Tonight* show in the absence of Johnny Carson, Lewis commented that while flying to New York he had used the restroom over Mississippi, fulfilling a long-standing ambition. Being offended by Lewis's remark, Governor John Bell Williams of Mississippi demanded that the National Broadcasting Company apologize. Lewis went back on the air on the *Tonight* show and said: "We did a joke which I suspect, in reflecting, wasn't terribly funny and we did offend some of our friends in Mississippi. I openly, publicly and humbly apologize. That certainly was not my intention . . . to offend." Despite the apology, WDAM-TV in Hattiesburg, Mississippi, announced the next day it was canceling the regular Tuesday night *Jerry Lewis Show* immediately. "We feel that the oral part of his apology last night would have been acceptable," said Marvin Reuben, vice-president and general manager, "had Mr. Lewis not cast doubt on his sincerity by a careless gesture at the end of his remarks."[11]

When you present your speech, use your face, your arms and hands, and your over-all bodily movements as communication agents. We are all aware of how vital facial expression can be in interpersonal communication, especially in conveying emotion. A wink, a raised eyebrow, an expression of pain, or a big smile tells people much. Descriptive gestures, as you discovered if you tried the experiment suggested above, are especially

[11] Reported in *The Kansas City Star*, March 26, 1969, p. 1.

helpful in describing things to people. Gestures may also be used to indicate the force of an idea. Therefore enlist them in making your ideas clear. Your arms and hands will talk quite freely if you just let them. How important a role gestures can play in public speaking is illustrated by a page-wide headline in a London newspaper when President Nixon visited in that country; the headline read: "The Talking Hands of President Nixon." It is reported that "When the President is driving home a point, his hands leap into action. They sweep and slide, slash and stab, solicit and supplicate. The fingers complete the gestures, alternately spread-eagling and folding to give his words emphasis. 'Dick's hands seem to be synchronized with his tongue,' said a friend." The same reporter also notes that Nixon uses "his hands to help form his thoughts point by point."[12]

Some general bodily movement, taking a few steps one way or another at appropriate moments—such as during transitions between thoughts—or taking a step or two forward or backward, will help you to convey your message to your listener. Be sure that any such movement is controlled and serves a useful purpose. Meaningless pacing tends to be distracting to the listener.

Herbert Spencer in his *Philosophy of Style* maintains that the objective of a good style is to so present a speech that it can be comprehended with the *least possible mental effort*. Since most people do not work hard at listening, we feel that Spencer's thought is critical to making ideas clear.

[12] "Nixon's Talking Hands," *Parade*, March 30, 1969, pp. 16–17.

4

be interesting

A country preacher once asked Henry Ward Beecher how to keep an audience awake on a hot Sunday afternoon, and Beecher told him to have an usher take a sharp stick and prod the preacher. Beecher's reply to his interrogator expresses the point of view of this chapter: It is the responsibility of the speaker to keep the audience awake. One may call a lack of attention bad listening, and it is, to an extent, since many people are notoriously poor listeners; yet the truth of the matter is that there is a direct correlation between the interest value of any speech and audience attention. As Sidney Smith has said, "Everything which is written [or spoken] is meant either to please or to instruct. This second object is difficult to effect without attending to the first." When you prepare a speech, place two signs in the fore of your mind, "Be imaginative! Be creative!" With the proper imagination, almost any speech topic can be made interesting and alive for an audience.

we must act

Few things appeal so much to people as action. Most of us would agree with Sophocles that "Heaven ne'er helps the men who will not act." Franklin D. Roosevelt knew the critical importance of action when he used it as his theme for his historic first inaugural address in 1933. These few words, "We must act," capsulized the desire of a nation made inert by history's greatest depression. The leaders of men have always been men of action. Theodore Roosevelt, John F. Kennedy, Douglas MacArthur, and Martin Luther King come to mind. Kim Giffin identifies five characteristics of the speaker that generate trust in his listeners. One of them is action. *"Dynamism* of the speaker as perceived by the listener," he says, "that is, communication behavior which appears to be more active than passive."[1] Quintilian, the Roman rhetorician, once was asked what he considered the three most essential components of effective speaking; he replied: "Action. Action. Action."

The speaker has two main sources of action to draw upon: energetic delivery and a lively style. Try to recall speakers whom you have considered unusually dull. Chances are they showed a total lack of animation in their presentation. Their actions seemed to say that they were not very interested in their subjects or in their audiences. By energetic delivery, we do not mean excessive table pounding, a high-pitched feverish voice, and all kinds of bodily contortions. We mean a delivery that has a sense of urgency and vitality about it. The speaker should give the listener visual cues that indicate he is vitally interested in his subject and that his speech is well worth listening to. The kind of bodily action we have in mind is typified by appropriate movement on the platform, spontaneous and meaningful gestures, and vocal vitality.

A dynamic verbal style is a second source of action. Read the speeches of history's great orators who held sway over popular audiences. You are likely to find yourself reading very rapidly and virtually breathless by the time you have finished. Their speeches are noted for movement and energy. Read Cicero and Demosthenes, Patrick Henry and Eugene Debs. Observe the energy that pulsates in the following passage from a speech by Wendell Phillips, a nineteenth century reform speaker:

[1] Kim Giffin, "The Contribution of Studies of Source Credibility to a Theory of Interpersonal Trust in the Communication Process," *Psychological Bulletin*, Vol. 68, No. 2 (1967), p. 107.

A chronic distrust of the people pervades the book-educated class of the North; they shrink from that free speech which is God's normal school for educating men, throwing upon them the grave responsibility of deciding great questions, and so lifting them to a higher level of intellectual and moral life. Trust the people—the wise and the ignorant, the good and the bad—with the gravest questions, and in the end you educate the race. At the same time you secure, not perfect institutions, not necessarily good ones, but the best institutions possible while human nature is the basis and the only material to build with.[2]

You may recall from your study of English grammar that sentences occur in the active or in the passive voice. The active voice means that the subject does the acting: "Bill broke down the gate." The passive voice means that the subject is acted upon: "The gate was broken down by Bill." It is easy to see how the active voice provides a greater amount of action. Things are happening in the sentence "Bill broke down the gate." Make a recording of your speech and analyze the amount of action you have in your sentences. If you find yourself speaking basically in the passive voice, try to restate your sentences so as to make more of them active. President Roosevelt did not say, "Action must be taken by us"; he said, "We must act."

don't talk about man; talk about a man

With this statement, E. B. White, the well-known writer, pinpoints the difference between dull and interesting speech. Attention-holding rhetoric deals with people who have names. All of us like stories. There may never have been a normal, healthy child who didn't like to hear stories. And although a lot

[2] Wendell Phillips, "The Scholar in a Republic," in *American Public Addresses, 1740–1952*, ed. A. Craig Baird (New York: McGraw-Hill Book Co., 1956), p. 153.

of adults don't like to read, they still enjoy stories. They go to movies and watch television. Doubtlessly stories have numerous factors that appeal to people, but one of the most important aspects is the hero, a person with thoughts and emotions who tries to cope with a series of problems that he encounters. Although an individual may often be used to symbolize or represent a large group of people, stories are never about a mass of people; they are about individuals with names who make up that mass of people.

Perhaps the most useful thing that a public speaker can do is to prepare an illustration file. Everyone of us comes across stories virtually every day that, if we noted them on cards and placed them in a properly indexed file, would be useful speech material at one time or another. Historical anecdotes, fictional episodes, newspaper reports, and even incidents reported to us orally, if they have strong human interest, can be used. Most good public speakers keep such a file; some of history's most successful orators had such a file ready at all times. There is probably not a successful preacher who does not have one or more books of collected illustrations on his desk and who does not maintain a personal resource file.

If you don't have a ready-made factual illustration handy for an important point in a speech, make one up. Most subjects have obvious plots around which a speaker can readily develop a hypothetical illustration. The little fellow who is struggling to make a living, the teenager who is wrestling with his conscience trying to decide between old and new values, the practical man who is able to simplify most of life's problems, the scientist who is desperately seeking answers to questions of great importance to human well-being—all these make natural hypothetical examples about specific persons.

The following two quotations are taken from student speeches. Both spoke on the same general value question, "What constitutes a full and meaningful life?" Both came to approximately the same conclusion in their search for an answer to the question. But notice the difference in the impact of their rhetoric; one uses a straightforward discussion of man in the abstract, and the other talks about specific persons.

Some men work for wealth; they yearn for wealth; they worship wealth; and in essence, they live for wealth. Others live for fame. Their primary concern is how well they are known and how long they will be remembered. As their final act they build monuments so that future generations will hold their name in awe. Another category is those people who live for a good time. But a good time is not an end in itself; it is a by-product of life, not a goal for living. In my opinion, financial success is not the true measure of a man. Neither are fame and high living the best yardsticks for measuring human life.

The best approach to evaluating the worth of a life is to ask the question, "How much did he contribute to life itself?" Did his existence do some good for other people? Did it further the ends of a good society? Was he more concerned with being a "man" in the true sense than with the acquisition of material goods that make for an easy life and an occasional good time? A person's life can only be judged to be full and meaningful in relation to how much he has contributed to life itself. No other criterion has lasting value.

Now read how the second student treated the same basic ideas and much of the same material.

We cannot deny that wealth, fame, and happiness have long been basic motivations for living. But how important are they? There is a biblical story told concerning an ancient Egyptian pharaoh who had wealth, fame, and happiness. His people decided to build a great monument to their king—one that would keep his name alive forever. It took many years and a great amount of money to erect the tribute. When at last the pyramid was finished, the people led the king to their achievement and awaited his reaction. The king recounted the great moments in the history of his country, and then with his hand pointed to the monument, he said, "This too shall pass away."

His words should be remembered by all of us, for they

apply to most of our monuments: the dollar, the famous name, and even our personal happiness. All these things, too, shall pass away. If these materialistic things are merely the transient marks of the living, what is the true mark of life, the measure of a man?

Perhaps I can best answer this question by telling a story. The story of Carl Sweeny, who graduated from Harvard University Medical School with honors. Friends and associates urged him to go to New York where he could unquestionably make a great deal of money and become famous. Instead, Carl Sweeny returned to his home town of Colony, Kansas. He called it the proudest moment of his life when he nailed up his first, and only, shingle, "Dr. Sweeny, Upstairs." For fifty years Dr. Sweeny practiced medicine in Colony, Kansas. In that time he delivered over 1,000 babies to the world, saved countless lives and shared the tears and the joys of his many friends. Carl Sweeny never became a rich man and his name is known to very few. When he died in 1931, the people of Colony wanted to build a lasting monument to mark his grave. But money was scarce in those depression years and a suitable stone seemed out of the question. Then someone suggested that they use the doctor's shingle to mark his grave. Today, if you go to the eastern outskirts of Colony, Kansas, you will find a small graveyard, and if you search closely enough, you will see a small rusted shingle bearing the inscription, "Dr. Sweeny, Upstairs."

Here was a man; his measure cannot be determined in fortune or fame. His measure includes those 1,000 births registered; those many lives saved and those countless joys and tears shared. The material monument to the Egyptian pharaoh did in time pass away, but the contribution of Dr. Carl Sweeny to himself and his friends, to Colony, Kansas, and to life shall never pass away. His was a life—the full measure of a life.

Don't forget about yourself as a source of illustrations. You have a name, a face, and a being for the audience. A story about yourself may exemplify E. B. White's advice to talk about *a* man perhaps better than any other approach. A personal anecdote will show involvement on your part and will probably enhance your credibility with the audience. Paul C. Harper, president of an advertising agency, began his speech "What's Happening, Baby?" by recalling a personal experience and thereby starting his speech at a concrete level.

A short time ago I was standing in a pub in London with one of my colleagues enjoying a beer. The name of the pub was "The King's Head and Eight Bells" and it is headquarters for the local pack of Mods. Four Mods were standing near us, two boy Mods in the new bell-bottom trousers and bee-waist coats—and two girl Mods with hair in their eyes. Then a fifth Mod with both bell-bottom trousers and hair in his eyes walked up and asked casually, "What's Happening, Baby?" As nearly as I can reconstruct it, the reply from one of the girls was, "Pip's topkick just gummed his mini. We all think that's fish."

After eavesdropping a little more, it became clear that what she was reporting was that Pip's father had removed his driving privileges, which they all thought was very stuffy. The meeting at the pub was a protest rally.

The language and problems of Teens are universal.

I am delighted to be standing here today for a number of reasons. First, I am glad to be able to pay my respects to this Club, which has achieved such a remarkable record of helping underprivileged young people. I understand the Club's work has been going on for 66 years—and so the Club's usefulness has withstood the severest test of all—the test of time. Second, I am particularly proud that advertising men have done so much to make the Club's program possible. It speaks well of our profession. And third, the whole subject of youth and its problems is a close one to me because there are six youths in our family, ages 9–18, 3 boys and 3 girls, and three of them teenagers—and while they do not classify as underprivileged —they do, of course, share in the real problems faced by all the youths of our time. Today let's focus on teenagers.[3]

[3] Paul C. Harper, "What's Happening, Baby?" *Vital Speeches of the Day*, Vol. 33 (November 1, 1966), p. 57. Reprinted by special permission.

be interesting

The audience, too, is a possible source of illustrations. Sometimes the most effective device is to say to your listeners, "Imagine yourself . . ." Observe how Cheri Tibbetts, a speech student, tried to get her audience to "feel" the plight of a slum child by using this device.

Imagine yourself a child of five. It is a hot day in July, and you're living in a dilapidated apartment house in the slums of a large city. The building is very hot and stuffy, you cannot feel the slightest breeze. Refuse lies in the hallways and on the stairs and there are flies all around it. In the air there is the smell of sour milk and the stench of wine. The walls of the building are made up of many cracks and holes. Your apartment includes a kitchen, with your mother and seven brothers and sisters. A bathroom down the hall serves your family as well as eight other families. Welfare is the source of support your family lives on. Your mother is an alcoholic and your father has not been home for several months. You're hungry and even the thought of bread and dry cereal which you've had for the past eight meals appeals to you. You haven't had a bath for several weeks and you are wearing the same clothes you wore a week ago. You are afraid to communicate with other people for you have never talked with anyone besides members of your own family. Because of all these factors you are a withdrawn, unhappy little person starved for affection.

Now you know how some children who are socially and economically deprived live. It is because of these children that Project Head Start was developed. Poverty's children are its most innocent, most helpless victims, but they are also more easily removed from its clutches. By meeting their need for attention and affection, by tending to medical needs that drain their energy, by opening their minds to the world of knowledge, we can set them on the road to successful lives. We can break the vicious cycle that would turn them into poverty's parents.

All the speakers quoted above have one thing in common: they follow E. B. White's advice to talk about *a* man in developing their subjects instead of about man in general. The first one used historical illustrations of an Egyptian pharaoh and Dr. Carl Sweeny, the second speaker took a slice from his own life to make his point, and the third one involved the listeners directly by getting them to play-act in their minds that they are slum children. There's nothing on earth that cannot be told through the eyes of a single individual. It's the classic formula; and it's the only one you can rely on to interest the average listener.

all the world's a stage

These words from Shakespeare's *As You Like It* may well embody some of the best advice a public speaker can find. Anyone who wants to act well the part of a person addressing an audience will employ dramatic elements in his presentation. We have already suggested two of these elements. action and the hero. An equally important one is dialogue. A seasoned speaker will not only turn much of his material into narrative but will also use dialogue to heighten the impact. Benjamin Franklin wrote: "Honest John Bunyan was the first that I know of who mixed narration and dialogue—a method of writing very engaging to the reader who in the most interesting parts finds himself, as it were, brought into the company and present at the discourse." This is equally true of public address.

Our history is filled with the names of orators who had that rare ability of capturing and swaying an audience. Some are well known, others are more obscure. One of the lesser known ones is a woman; a woman who spent nearly fifty years of her life giving speeches, often giving as many as eight a day. Her life consisted virtually of giving speeches. She was Dr. Anna Howard Shaw, a woman suffragist, who campaigned throughout the Union for woman's right to vote. Men and women alike readily agreed that she could hold the attention of her listeners. Her speeches were packed with action, with narrative—and with dialogue. Observe her technique in talking about an antisuffragist who boasted that she was a Daughter of the American Revolution:

I was met by one of these daughters once who asked me why I spent all my time in the furtherance of the woman-suffrage movement and why I did not join their society. She said, "Were not your ancestors in the Revolution?" I replied they were, and I added, "And they fought hard, but they fought on the wrong side." She said, "I am so sorry for you. Why, are you not sorry that your ancestors were on the wrong side?" I told her that I have had such a hard time getting on the right side and keeping there I have had no time to worry over my great-grandfather. I added, "It does not matter half so much to me where my grandfather stood as where I stand, and the difference between you and me, my dear friend, is that you stand where my great-grandfather stood, and I stand where yours stood."

The lady did not like it. She did not like my reference to my grandfather. She said, "I descended from a long line of Revolutionary ancestors." I answered, "Yes, that is exactly what you have done; you have *descended* from a long line of Revolutionary ancestors; and I have *ascended* from a line of Revolutionary ancestors, and I would rather ascend from my ancestors than descend from them any time."

That is just the trouble with a great many people who catch a glimpse of a sublime idea. They fail to make its application to everyday life. If these excellent ladies would make that application to everyday life for just one moment, they would see the inconsistency of opposing the fundamental principles of democracy and the fundamental principles in whose defense their ancestors died.

the old in the new is what claims attention

William James, the world-renowned psychologist, once wrote: "It is an odd circumstance that neither the old nor the new, by itself, is interesting: the absolutely old is insipid; the absolutely new makes no appeal at all. The old *in* the new is what claims attention—the old with a slightly new turn." All of us have had the experience of being some considerable distance from home and seeing an automobile with license plates from our home county and immediately waving at the occupants or even addressing them warmly if the opportunity arises. Yet if we met these total strangers in our home state we would find nothing interesting about them; we would ignore them as usual. A listening audience behaves similarly. It will ignore and find boring what is already well known if it is presented in the usual manner. On the other hand, old ideas presented in a new and somewhat novel way will hold attention. People want new approaches and novel insights to old ideas.

How would you like to be assigned the task of giving a speech on "The Wedding Ceremony"? Unimaginative speakers would be sure to give a dull and uninspiring speech on this subject. Yet this was the problem confronting a high school girl named Donna Lasseter from Olathe, Kansas, at an informative speaking contest. Let's see what she did with the subject by examining a major portion of her speech.

Every now and then you read in the papers about a bride who has gotten married in a mini-skirt or bell bottom pants. Recently, in Kansas City, a couple was married yogi style. Another couple took their vows in the middle of a parachute jump.

Naturally, clergymen take a dim view of this so-called sacrilege. They say that it introduces paganism and secularism to a very solemn and religious ceremony. However, this argument is not really correct, for if you examine the traditional type of wedding service, you find that the only part that is religious is the vows themselves. The rest has been derived from barbaric customs and superstitions. For example, we assume that the purpose of the best man is to witness. But it didn't start that way. To find the origin of this custom, we must go back to the time when the institution of marriage was very young. Among the cave-dwellers and the tribesmen, one of the strongest taboos was that against incest. To avoid incest, a man had to find a bride from a tribe other than his own, since he was usually related to every girl in his tribe. But usually these tribes were warring against each other, so the man had to steal a bride, thus provoking an attack. He couldn't do this alone, so he picked the strongest and bravest man in the tribe: in other words, the best man. But sometimes the opposition looked a little too rough for just two men, so the groom drafted a near army of men. These were the first groomsmen.

Of course, helping to capture a bride was a nasty job, and it wouldn't be for the benefit of either the best man or the groomsmen, for they wouldn't get the girl. The groom had to make it worth their while. He would bribe each one of his helpers with a small gift: usually a fur or a semiprecious stone. And today, etiquette still demands that the groom give a gift to those who stand up for him. In the process of this capture, the bride was very likely to be roughed up. Since she was to be his property, naturally he didn't want her damaged in any way. After all, if he decided to dissolve the marriage, he would get a better price for her if she were undamaged. So he would wrap her up in a blanket before carrying her off. This was the first veil. You can see that this veil has long outlived its purpose. This is because many superstitious tribes believed that evil spirits would invade the bride's body unless she was covered. So this is why we have retained the veil for all of these years.

After a man had succeeded in capturing a girl, he would take her immediately back to his own tribe. There a ceremony would take place before evil spirits could harm the girl. The first service was really a series of incantations to ward off evil spirits and to invoke the blessings of the gods of fertility.

But at this ceremony further complications developed, for the bride didn't want to get married. She would become the slave of the man she married, so she would put up quite a fight. The groom would have to tie the girl's wrists, not only during the service, but for some time afterward, until she was used to being a captive. This was the first "marriage bond." Later in man's history this was no longer necessary, but for some reason man liked to put the woman in a subordinate position. So he would symbolically tie her wrists by placing a bracelet over her arm. She would wear this as long as the marriage lasted. It is probably by feminine persuasion that this bracelet was reduced to a band of gold, and this is how we got the wedding ring.

After the ceremony it is traditional to go on a honeymoon. This is a very romantic tradition that began in the most unromantic way, for it used to be a sign of cowardice on the part of the groom. With his newly acquired in-laws advancing very rapidly, sometimes the groom would take his bride and hide out for a period of time. By the time that the moon had gone through all of its phases, it was considered safe to come back out of hiding. And this was the first honeymoon.

Naturally, a system of marriage such as this could not last forever. It was too dangerous for all concerned. A compromise had to be reached. Sometimes a man would bribe the parents of the girl to hold off the attack. Eventually, these arrangements were made in advance, and so man arrived to the level of marriage by purchase. It worked like this: A father legally owned his daughter until he wanted her to get married. He would sell her to the highest bidder. Whoever paid the right price not only became her owner, but her husband as well.

This system of marriage brought along its own traditions. For example, the father still gives away the bride at the wedding ceremony. Also, the marriage certificate originated during this time. The first certificate was signed only by the girl's father, the groom, and two witnesses, since the bride was only considered a piece of property. The first wedding certificate was really the receipt for the sale of the daughter.

We can see that there are many things in the modern wedding service that are only symbolic of earlier, more barbaric times. However, today the wedding ceremony is considered relatively safe. All of the parties involved have benefited from this refinement, but there is one person who has benefited more than all the rest. This is the present-day mother-in-law. For if today's mother-in-law were to take a trip back in time, she might find herself to be the main attraction of a bridal feast, for many cannibalistic tribes believed that the secret of a happy marriage was to eat the bride's mother on the wedding night.

We can turn the principle "the old in the new is what claims attention" around and also say that new ideas hung on familiar pegs interest an audience. The completely new is alien to our experience and we find it difficult to grasp. This is not to say that we are not interested in new things, for we surely are, as is witnessed by our desire for all kinds of new adventures. It is just that our interest basically stems from finding the familiar in the unfamiliar or the old in the new. If the new is related to what the listener has seen, heard, read, felt, believed, or done, which still exists in his consciousness and in his knowledge, the message will become real to him. In other words, the speaker must place totally new information and new ideas into the listener's life.

i was born to laughter and merry comrades make me glow

Humor has always been a tremendous interest device in a speech. Not that great speeches can't be given without humor, nor that all outstanding public speakers have been competent humorists, but that almost all speeches, except those constrained by the solemnity of the occasion, profit from humorous material. Most members of an audience would agree with William Rose Benét that merry comrades make them glow. Two of the greatest speakers of our time, Adlai Stevenson and John F. Kennedy, used humor extensively. Stevenson's wit was so sharp in the 1952 presidential campaign that his opponents felt compelled to make an attack on it. Newsmen enjoyed President Kennedy's press conferences as they had never enjoyed press conferences before because of the President's witty repartee.

We are not trying to say that every speech should be opened with two or three of the latest jokes the speaker has heard. In fact, this practice has become so ritualistic that it sometimes is embarrassing, especially if the jokes are old, irrelevant, or in bad taste. Be wary of the latest jokes (or for that matter old ones) because the audience is likely to have already heard them. Moreover, the latest jokes seldom pertain to the speaker's subject and we feel that all humor in a speech should further the basic message; sometimes it can be used even for making a quite serious point. Hardly anything is worse than humor out of taste for a particular audience. If you have any question about the taste of a piece of humor, don't use it, for if you have reservations about it, some members of the audience will be sure to have also.

It is a mistake to believe that speeches should begin on a humorous note—with an "attention getter"—and then be deadly serious from that point on. Actually, the speaker is very likely to have excellent attention during the first five minutes of his speech; after that point attention tends to become a problem. "Merry glows" wear off fast. It is thus useful to sprinkle humor throughout the speech instead of concentrating it all at the first.

by delight, we all quote

Ralph Waldo Emerson, himself often quoted, realized that speakers and writers take great delight in using short quotations; perhaps with some justification, because a short quotation, aptly chosen and skillfully used, adds impact and interest to a speaker's ideas. Adlai Stevenson and the Kennedys made frequent and effective use of this technique. Stevenson, for example, generated interest in a speech to Radcliffe College girls by beginning with a short quotation: "Nietzsche said that women were God's second mistake." Later in the speech, he said: "Dr. Johnson wrote, that one of the last things we men are willing to give up, even in advanced age, is the supposition that we have something to say of interest to the opposite sex." Robert F. Kennedy told his Berlin audience, "The Atlantic Nations must constantly renew the vitality of the institutions which brought success yesterday. In politics as in biology, to endure we must evolve. 'He who moves not forward,' wrote Goethe, 'goes backward.'" President John F. Kennedy had a fondness for the short quotation also and used it to good effect. For example, he told a commencement audience at American University: "Professor Woodrow Wilson once said that every man sent out from a university should be a man of his nation as well as a man of his time and I'm confident that the men and women who carry the honor of graduating from this institution will continue to give from their lives, from their talents a high measure of public service and public support." Later in the speech, he said: "'There are few earthly things more beautiful than a university,' wrote John Masefield, in his tribute to English universities—and his words are equally true today. He did not refer to towers or to campus. He admired the splendid beauty of a university, because it was, he said, 'a place where those who hate ignorance may strive to know, where those who perceive truth may strive to make others see.'"

The Bible is a frequent source for effective short quotations. President Kennedy in his American University address said: "'When a man's ways please the Lord, he maketh even his enemies to be at peace with him'" (Proverbs 16:17); and in his renowned inaugural address: "Let both sides unite to heed in all corners of the earth the command of Isaiah: to 'undo the heavy burdens . . . (and) let the oppressed go free'" (Isaiah 58:6).

Quotations must be chosen with care, lest they produce tedium rather than delight. Generally speaking, they should: (1) state a thought in a striking manner; (2) be short and concise; (3) be relatively fresh in their usage, instead of tired and shopworn; (4) fit the thought precisely and not be dragged into the speech because they appeal to the speaker.

It is not necessary that the exact words always be used; a reference to someone's words can often be effective, as is done by Adlai Stevenson in the following: "Thomas Jefferson proclaimed that the United States was the strongest nation on earth not because of its military might or its productive capacity, but because of its revolutionary ideas." And again, "Chesterton once said that the trouble with truisms is that they are still true."

The story is told that when a certain speech was called to the attention of Charles James Fox, the great eighteenth century British parliamentary debater, he responded: "Did the speech read well when reported? If so, it was a bad one." Fox undoubtedly was observing that good speeches have a distinctive *oral* quality. We do not agree with Fox that all good speeches read badly, but we do contend that good prose writing does not necessarily constitute a good speech.

Speeches, with rare exception, are created for the moment of presentation. They are not designed to produce great literature for the ages; they are designed to effect immediate instruction or persuasion. The public speaker meets his audience face-to-face and talks to them. Such direct address creates a relationship between communicator and receiver that does not exist in written communication. Whereas the writer may speak in an indirect manner, the speaker is always "I," the audience is "you," and collectively they are "we." Since a cardinal principle of effective public speaking is audience involvement, the speaker will want to make ample use of personal pronouns, for such direct address will generate and hold attention. Observe how Newton Minow, in his now famous address to the National Association of Broadcasters on "Television: The Vast Wasteland," makes use of this technique: (The italics are ours.)

It would not surprise *me* if some of *you* have expected *me* to come here today and say in effect, "Clean up *your* own house or the government will do it for *you*."

Well, in a limited sense, *you* would be right—*I've* just said it.

But *I* want to say to *you* earnestly that it is not in that spirit that *I* come before *you* today, nor is it in that spirit that *I* intend to serve the FCC.[4]

in short measures life may perfect be

At a dinner meeting at which Will Rogers, the renowned humorist, was toastmaster, several speakers were scheduled to address the audience and they agreed to make short presentations that would not exceed eight minutes. But one man went on for forty-five minutes and wound up saying, "Mr. Toastmaster, I'm sorry if I overstayed my time, but I left my watch at home." Will Rogers leaned forward, and said in a friendly tone, "There was a calendar right behind you."

Research shows that listeners' attention wavers badly after the first fifteen minutes. It is thus safe to say that poor communication often results from a speech that lasts forty-five minutes or more. Obviously the interest value of a speech strongly influences how well people are able to listen, and they may find it easier to pay attention to an interesting forty-five-minute presentation than to a dull and listless fifteen-minute performance. Nevertheless, people will probably get as much from most twenty-minute speeches as they will from sixty-minute presentations. The message is clear: Don't talk too long. There is, however, a correlative thought, equally important. The longer your speech is going to be the greater need for interest materials. It may be altogether possible to make a three- or four-minute presentation with little interest value and have most of the audience tuned in to the speaker. But it is almost sure that most of them will be on another channel if that speech is extended to an hour's duration without an equal increase in interest factors.

While short speeches are not always the best, the best

[4] Newton N. Minow, "A Vast Wasteland," *The New York Times*, May 10, 1961, p. 79.

speeches always seem short. Consider the banquet speaker who spoke for what seemed like days to some of his listeners. Finally, one suffering auditor, leaving by a side door, encountered another member of the audience who had preceded him. "Has he finished yet?" the earlier deserter asked. "Yes," was the reply. "He finished long ago; but he won't stop."

We agree with Irvin Cobb's classic remark: "No speech can be entirely bad if it is short enough." Ben Jonson quite aptly discerned:

> In small proportions we just beauties see,
> And in short measures life may perfect be.

5

be believable

If you want to anger a person, writes Irving Lee, contradict him, tell him that what he is saying is not true.[1] Clearly, all of us, when we speak of things to which we are committed, want to be believed. "Whoever believes any thing," as Montaigne pointed out long ago, "thinks it a deed of charity to persuade another to believe it." Few things are as frustrating as having our charitable acts repudiated by those at whom they are directed.

Nevertheless, for the public speaker, there is an important difference between *being believed* and *being believable*. Aristotle noted this difference more than two thousand years ago when he observed that the goal of the rhetorician is not simply to persuade but to be able to determine "the available means of persuasion." This approach can be likened to that of a doctor treating a patient. We do not expect that a doctor will be able to cure every sick person he treats; such expectation would be unreasonable since some people are too ill to recover. What we do expect of a doctor is that he use every means available to medical science to place the patient back on the road to good health.

Similarly, no speaker can reasonably expect each member of his audience to accept everything he has to say. The beliefs of the speaker and the listener may, in some instances, be too far apart to be reconciled—at least during a single persuasive effort. This may be true in spite of the rightness of our cause

[1] Irving J. Lee, *How to Talk with People* (New York: Harper & Row, 1952), pp. 27–28.

or the irrefutability of our arguments, for there is often little relationship between the depth and the rationality of a person's beliefs. James Harvey Robinson put it well when he observed: "We are incredibly heedless in the formation of our beliefs, but find ourselves filled with illicit passion for them when anyone proposes to rob us of their companionship."

Although, from a realistic point of view, we cannot expect always to be believed, the aim of every public speaker should be always to be believable. This is true regardless of our goal in speaking. Whether our purpose in speaking is to promote action, form attitudes, or simply to impart information, we wish in each instance to present our message in a way that is believable.

With a little thought, it soon becomes clear that in public speaking believability is closely related to the source of the message. Because in written communication the source is often obscured, the reader tends to react directly to the message itself with little or no regard for the source. In public speaking, however, where the speaker is both physically and psychologically at "center stage," this is simply not possible. In the public speaking situation the message is inextricably mediated by the speaker as a person and, consequently, the communicator's image assumes great significance.

believability and the speaker's image

The following is part of a report written by one of our students:

Len was a classmate of mine in a college course in group discussion. During several meetings of our group he developed a reputation for being something of a joker. He seemed to have a supply of stories for every occasion, he was quick with a quip or pun, and in general seemed to be a loose, easy-going kind of guy. With Len around, we all knew things were never going to get too tense, even when the issues we were discussing were pretty controversial. The only trouble with him was that he sometimes carried the humor too far and we didn't get as much done as we should have. But this was a fairly minor fault and we all tended to overlook it; as one of the members expressed it, "Len is just that kind of person."

It was during a discussion of Medicare one day, while we all seemed in general agreement that doctors' bills were getting too high, that Len broke in with the exclamation: "You people are all crazier than hell!" The remark, coming as it did, struck us as sort of funny and got a few chuckles. When he shot back with the charge, "You're nothing but a bunch of communists," the laughter got louder since everybody knew that "good old Len" was putting us on. Finally, when Len leaped to his feet and yelled, "Dammit, I'm serious," most of us almost fell out of our chairs in hysterics.

It took a while, but we finally got the message—*Len was really serious!* As we discovered later, he had a real hang-up on this particular issue (both his father and older brother were doctors) that none of us had known about. At any rate, the whole thing was a big shock and our discussion broke down completely. I think it's accurate to say that our group was never quite the same again.

We had come to think of Len in such a way that we expected everything he said to be a joke—we just couldn't believe it when he was serious. Because of the "blow-up," we've developed a whole new image of him. He's still the group joker, but now we know that he has a serious side, too.

Aristotle concluded, as the above story illustrates, that the speaker's image—which he termed *ethos*—was probably the most significant determinant of his believability. If anything, image has taken on an even more important role in contemporary events. News commentator Eric Sevareid, in discussing the 1968 Presidential campaign, observed that a candidate's success had long been thought to hinge on three factors— party, program, and personality. However, as party loyalty has faded and programs have merged, personality has become most important. "Trust," he concluded, "trust in a man has become the final arbiter."[2]

The importance of the relationship between image and believability can best be demonstrated, perhaps, by what happens when the image turns bad. The phrase "credibility gap" has assumed a permanent place in our national vocabulary because the image of one man, Lyndon Johnson, became unbelievable. Because of this turn in his image President Johnson found his ability to communicate meaningfully with his constituency almost totally impaired, and it eventually influenced him in deciding not to seek a second term in office.

We know that our image of a person determines how we feel about him and act toward him. But what is it that determines our image of him in the first place? Although this question can, perhaps, never be completely answered, we can point to some determining factors that are of concern to the public speaker.

It may be well to begin by acknowledging that there are some determinants of his image that the speaker will be unable to influence. In fact, there are some that he will not even know of. Past actions, of course, can't be changed. For this reason, Aristotle excluded reputation from his treatment of rhetoric. But even if past actions can't be changed, reputation can be taken into account, and perhaps modified, by the public speaker. Evangelist Billy Graham, for example, knows that he is generally perceived in a certain—often negative—way by the students and faculties of state universities and he adapts his speaking to these groups on the basis of that knowledge. This was demonstrated in the speech of Graham's quoted in Chapter 2.

A speaker should also be aware that his image is likely to be affected by factors of which, because they are irrational, he may have no awareness. As Arthur Cohen, a behavioral scientist, has pointed out:

[2] Eric Sevareid, "Campaign '68," Columbia Broadcasting System, November 3, 1968.

Both relevant and irrelevant aspects of credibility determine change of attitude; audiences are not composed of people who respond only to the objectively relevant aspects of a communicator. Thus, for example, whether a person is effective may depend on whether he is perceived as an expert, but also on whether he is fat, sloppy, neat, ugly, handsome, a poor athlete, or a member of a minority group.[3]

In addition to reputation and the irrational as determinants of image, the audience's perception of a speaker is significantly influenced by many factors he is able to control within the speaking situation itself. The remainder of this chapter, therefore, will deal with the relationship between a speaker's message and the relevant images held by his audience.

messages and images

Eminent philosopher and economist Kenneth Boulding has written extensively on the image.

[An image] is what I believe to be true; my subjective knowledge . . . The image is built up as a result of all past experiences of the possessor of the image. . . . Every time a message reaches him his image is likely to be changed in some degree by it, and as his image is changed his behavior patterns will be changed likewise.

We must distinguish carefully between the image and the messages that reach it. The messages consist of *information* in the sense that they are structured experiences. *The meaning of a message is the change which it produces in the image.*[4]

[3] Arthur R. Cohen, *Attitude Change and Social Influence* (New York: Basic Books, 1964), pp. 28–29.

[4] Kenneth Boulding, *The Image* (Ann Arbor: University of Michigan Press, 1956), pp. 6–7.

All sorts of images may be pertinent to the success of any given speech. These include, for example, the speaker's images of his audience, the occasion, himself, his purpose in speaking, and even the function of public speaking in general. Many of these speaker-oriented images have been dealt with in earlier chapters. Of the relevant images held by the audience, two, it seems to us, should be of most concern to a speaker—its image of him and its image of the central purpose of his speech. As we discussed in Chapter 2, the speaker's chances for success are closely tied to his ability to discern and adapt to the essential images held by his audience.

when messages hit images

When a message—either verbal or nonverbal—sent by the speaker hits an image held by his audience one of three things can happen.[5] To begin with, the image may remain largely unchanged. Regrettably, this is the case with much public speaking. The audience sees the speaker and hears him talking, but the listeners know that they are witnessing a perfunctory response to some occasion (perhaps a class assignment). The fact that the speaker is now in front of the room talking does little to change their images one way or the other. If the speaker should not show up when scheduled to speak, however, or if he should speak in a way contrary to the listeners' expectations, these messages *would* tend to alter the audience's images. In this sense, certain kinds of speeches may be significant in their relationship to audience expectation, even when meaningless in any larger sense.

Adding to, or clarifying (or, perhaps, subtracting from, or confusing), is a second way that messages can affect images. We recall, for example, listening to a speech which analyzed the relationship of inflation to the cost of living. The speaker, in this case, added something to our image of this phenome-

---

[5] The following discussion of the effect of messages on images is based in part on Kenneth Boulding's *The Image*, pp. 7–13.

non, but he did not cause us to substantially revise it. Our picture, both of economists and of the influence of inflation and cost of living, had been clarified but not fundamentally revised.

Occasionally, however, images do undergo revolutionary change. This, though it may not happen often, is the third kind of impact that messages can have on images. Boulding provided an example:

> A man, for instance, may think himself a pretty good fellow and then hear a preacher who convinces him that, in fact, his life is worthless and shallow, as he is presently living it. The words of the preacher cause a radical reformulation of the man's image of himself in the world, and his behavior changes accordingly.[6]

messages and images in conflict

It is this final situation, where messages are inconsistent with images, that provides a speaker with his greatest difficulty. An image, Boulding tells us, "is in itself resistant to change. When it receives messages which conflict with it, its first impulse is to reject them as in some sense untrue."[7]

In approaching situations of this kind, the speaker must, if he is to be effective, recognize the relationship between idea and speaker images. As we pointed out earlier in the chapter, because of the public speaker's extreme visibility, he invariably acts as a mediator of the ideational dimension of the speech.

when you like the speaker but not his ideas

A speaker who is able to project a believable image will enhance the chance that an unpopular idea will be accepted. Thus, when Cassius Clay (Muhammad Ali), the heavyweight boxing champion, appeared at a meeting attended largely by Christian black students he was able to create audience attitudes favorable to his non-Christian Black Muslim religion.

[6] Boulding, p. 8.
[7] Boulding, p. 8.

Additionally, his conduct during the speech contributed even more to the audience's image of him as a believable speaker. It is important to note here that even if the audience had remained unmoved by his appeal on behalf of the Black Muslim religion, Muhammad Ali's personal image would probably have been maintained or enhanced by the messages he sent.

Although a favorable speaker image can enhance an unpopular idea, a speaker must be careful not to overestimate the potency of his personal appeal when advocating ideas inconsistent with those of the audience. Just as a favorable speaker image can make an unpopular idea less unpopular under some circumstances, under other circumstances the association with such an idea can destroy an audience's favorable image of a speaker. As Samuel Johnson once put it, "Every man who attacks my belief diminishes in some degree my confidence in it, and therefore makes me uneasy, and I am angry with him who makes me uneasy."

when you like the ideas but not the speaker

As we have just discussed, a speaker's image may suffer if he associates himself with an unpopular idea with which the audience is sufficiently ego-involved. But the opposite may also be true—a speaker may successfully build a favorable image by associating himself with an idea that is at once both important to, and popular with, his audience. Such a case occurred during Democrat Edmund Muskie's 1968 campaign for the Vice-Presidency. The following story was originated by *The New York Times* News Service:

> Sen. Edmund S. Muskie (D-Me.) startled a rally in front of the soot-blackened old Washington courthouse yesterday, including 30 or 40 noisy anti-war protesters, by inviting a young heckler to share the platform with him. . . .
>
> While the crowd grumbled, the senator leaned forward and said he would let the students send a representative to the podium to speak for them. . . .
>
> At that, Richard Brady, a 21-year-old senior English major

from Massapequa, N.Y., pushed through the crowd and mounted the platform. . . .

"It's like this," said Brady, who wore a khaki shirt, levis and sandals, his black hair long and uncombed. "Everybody calls us dirty and unwashed."

The partisan crowd, made up mostly of older people, booed loudly. . . .

Brady continued: "You guys say we are dirty and unwashed. We are the true Americans. We love the flag just as everyone else. We want America to stand for what the constitution stands for, which is everyone is equal under the law, which is not true in this country."

As cheers rang out, he went on. . . .[8]

It's clear that, at the time he began to speak, Mr. Brady's image with the audience of "older people" was not good. He was a war protester and a heckler, he dressed like a hippie, and his hair was "long and uncombed." When he was asked to speak, the "crowd grumbled"; when he began to speak the crowd "booed loudly." Yet, after he identified himself with "true Americans," love of the flag, the Constitution, and equality for all, he was cheered. Mr. Brady was able to improve his image by associating himself with some of the most powerful "god terms" of this culture.

Since we have now discussed the relationship between image and believability, we will move on to consider those messages most influential in developing images of believability.

messages of believability

There are, as we have discovered, many factors that influence the listeners' perceptions of a speaker and his ideas. Of all these, however, none are more significant as means of affecting audience images than the four major message categories we will describe in the following pages.

[8] *The Kansas City Times*, September 26, 1968, pp. 1A and 13A.

Kenneth Burke, a well-known rhetorical theorist, has said, "You persuade a man only insofar as you can talk his language by speech, gesture, tonality, order, image, attitude, idea, *identifying* your ways with his."[9] With Burke, we feel that identification is both one of the most common and most effective messages of believability. It's true that we tend to perceive those who are like us as understanding us and having our best interests at heart.

Messages of identification, as Burke notes, can be sent through many media, including how one dresses and the words one uses. The late Senator Robert Kerr of Oklahoma, for example, is reputed to have exchanged his business suit for work coveralls when he campaigned in the rural areas of his state.[10] Another Middle Western senator, a man who graduated with top honors from his law school, has not forgotten to talk about his "daddy" and his "mamma" when addressing the folks back home.

The most common medium for messages of identification, however, is not dress or speech mannerism, but the ideas and values one expresses. Former Vice-President Hubert Humphrey, a knowledgeable and experienced public speaker, demonstrated this well in an address at the convention of the National Association for the Advancement of Colored People in 1966. At a time when some Negroes were beginning to reject white involvement in their cause, Mr. Humphrey made sure that he was clearly identified with his audience:

America is marching on the road to freedom.
I am proud to be back among my friends of the NAACP who have led this march for 57 years.
From the shadows of a dark past toward the shining hope

---

[9] Kenneth Burke, *A Grammar of Motives and a Rhetoric of Motives* (Cleveland: World Publishing Co., 1962), p. 579.

[10] William B. English, "Robert S. Kerr: A Study in Ethos" (Ph.D. dissertation, University of Oklahoma, 1966).

of a brighter tomorrow, this march has been difficult, uncertain, and often dangerous. But history shall surely record its glory.

For we marched . . . even when our band was small and our ranks thin and ragged . . . even when victory seemed a distant and unattainable goal.

There have been young marchers and old . . . Negro and white . . . rich and poor . . . but always marching with a common spirit—moved by a common hope—and striving for a common objective.

We marched and fought against separate and unequal education, and segregated lunch counters, and a seat in the back of the bus. . . .

We have learned. . . .

We are here today. . . .

Our triumphs have been impressive and numerous.[11]

No one listening to this introduction to Mr. Humphrey's speech could forget that he had been a friend to the Negro well before "racial liberalism" became a popular stance.

The late Malcolm X, although a Negro himself, faced his own image problem in addressing a black audience gathered in Cleveland's Cory Methodist Church in April of 1964. Malcolm, an ex-convict and now identified with Black Muslimism, was attempting to win over a predominantly Christian audience to his ideas of black nationalism. His listeners, initially suspicious of both the man and the militancy of his plan, soon found themselves thoroughly identified with both. Here is a short section of that speech:

Although I'm still a Muslim, I'm not here tonight to discuss my religion. I'm not here to try and change your religion. I'm not here to argue or discuss anything that we differ about, because it's time for us to submerge our differences and realize that it is best for us to first see that we have the same problem, a common problem—a problem that will make you

[11] *Congressional Record*, July 12, 1966, pp. A3607–A3609.

catch hell whether you're a Baptist, or a Methodist, or a Muslim, or a nationalist. Whether you're educated or illiterate, whether you live on the boulevard or in the alley, you're going to catch hell just like I am. We're all in the same boat and we all are going to catch the same hell from the same man. He just happens to be a white man. All of us have suffered here, in this country, political oppression at the hands of the white man, economic exploitation at the hands of the white man, and social degradation at the hands of the white man.[12]

In focusing on the abuse *all* blacks have been subjected to by white society, Malcolm X effectively demonstrates Eric Hoffer's conclusion that "hatred is the most accessible and comprehensive of all unifying agents."[13]

The use of identification as a means of establishing a believable image is not confined to controversial issues and highly charged situations. Bill Gove, a man who earns his living as a public speaker, customarily devotes an extensive period at the outset of each speech exclusively to the purpose of achieving a close rapport with his listeners. His approach to the problem is illustrated in the following section of a speech he delivered to a sales convention in St. Paul, Minnesota.

> Thank you—Thank you, Dave, for that fine introduction. I'm glad you mentioned the wedding, Dave, and I'm glad you mentioned Nancy. I'm thrilled that Nancy—my daughter Nancy—and my new son-in-law to be are here sitting down in front. Incidentally, he's a salesman with McGill-Warner. . . .
>
> It's wonderful to be here. . . . I remember when I was selling vacuum cleaners back in the early depression. We used to have sales meetings where we would march around the table every morning singing "Rise Up Ye Men of Hoover."

[12] *Malcolm X Speaks*, copyright © 1965 by Merit Publishers and Betty Shabazz. From *Malcolm X Speaks*, ed. George Breitman (New York: Grove Press, 1965), p. 24.

[13] Eric Hoffer, *The True Believer* (New York: Harper & Row, 1951), p. 89.

And then we'd go out through an open door and the boss would hit us across the fanny with a copy of the morning paper and say "go out and get 'em."

Gove continued in this vein for several minutes, interspersing stories of his own experiences *as a salesman* with jokes *about salesmen*, until there could be no doubt in the listeners' minds that this man was one of them.

An examination of any effective public speech will reveal that the speaker has successfully formulated and transmitted messages that in some way identified him with his audience. Although it may be that the impulse to identify is almost instinctive with people in communication situations, messages, to be successful, must be made to fit the situation and the audience, as well as the speaker himself. What is appropriate for Malcolm X speaking to a black audience on the subject of black nationalism, for example, cannot be expected to fit a college student speaking in a classroom, even if he should decide to deal with the same subject. The construction of messages of identification cannot be formularized; each of us must develop the ability to analyze our individual situations if we are to determine appropriate means of identifying with those whom we seek to have listen to us.

qualify your right to speak

An image of believability requires some sort of message that effectively answers the following question: What quality, knowledge, ability, or experience do you have which qualifies you to speak to us on this subject? Acceptable qualifications may range widely. In one instance a speaker may be acceptable to his audience simply because of the intensity of his feeling; in another case such acceptance may require special training or achievement. But in every circumstance, the speaker must first determine what kind of qualification messages will have an impact on his listeners' images of him, and second, make sure that those messages are transmitted.

One reason why we have stressed repeatedly that a speaker should talk about things drawn from his personal experience —things that make a difference to him—is that if he does he will find it much easier to formulate and send messages of qualification. A speaker cannot, however, assume that simply *being qualified* to speak is synonymous with *being perceived* by an audience as qualified to speak. Failure to send this message is a common fault of beginning speakers.

While teaching public speaking at the U.S. Army's Command and General Staff College, we came across a case that illustrates the above point perfectly. A young major had given a speech analyzing the nature of Soviet influence in the world and predicting the direction of that influence during the next several years. By most conventional standards, it was an excellent speech. The subject was timely and significant to the audience—his classmates. Evidence was used extensively; the development of ideas was clear; and the delivery was fluent and varied. The only thing wrong was that during the discussion following the speech the speaker was severely criticized. Although the critics were not precise in pinpointing what they disliked, they were almost unanimous in pronouncing it a "poor speech." Later, after some questioning, it became clear that the audience didn't accept the major's right to deal with this specialized topic, let alone to make predictions about the future. "After all," they declared, "he's just a student like the rest of us." What the major had neglected to tell his listeners was that he had almost completed a doctorate in Soviet Area studies, that he had lived in Russia for a period of several years, and that he spoke Russian fluently.

Establishing one's qualification can be accomplished subtly; in fact, it ought to be. As Quintilian, the famous rhetorician of ancient Rome, put it, "The perfection of art is to conceal art." In other words, effective messages of qualification can be sent without the speaker sounding like a braggart. In the case of the major, for example, his speech might have begun like this:

My father, like almost every one of us in this room, is an Army officer, although he's now retired. As your children can tell you, being an "Army brat" has both its advantages and its disadvantages. But for me one of the big advantages came during my high school years when my father was assigned as military aide to our ambassador in Russia. During the four years we lived in the Soviet Union I came to know something of its history, its language, and its people. And I became intensely interested in the political role this nation was playing in the modern world. That's why I would like to talk today about . . .

As you can see, there is nothing magic about this opening. There are other ways that would be equally, if not more, effective. Still, if the major's speech had opened in a way something like the introduction we have suggested, he probably could have avoided most of the negative reaction to his speech. Without this information he simply wasn't believable on the subject he had chosen to deal with.

One normally can't determine by looking at a person that he has lived in a certain place, speaks a certain language, or has studied for a doctorate. There are, however, qualification messages that are both nonverbal and conspicuous. Such was the case with Ralph Zimmermann, a speaker who wore braces and walked with a limp.

Ralph was a student at Wisconsin State College at Eau Claire at a time when one of the authors was attending St. Olaf College in Northfield, Minnesota. Because the schools are not far apart and since we were both intercollegiate debaters, we competed in many of the same debate tournaments. Mr. Zimmermann was a hemophiliac and he wrote a speech about that disease which won the Interstate Oratorical Contest.

Although the signs of Ralph Zimmermann's physical affliction were unmistakable as he rose from his chair and made his way to the podium, he was a skilled enough speaker to know that on the subject of hemophilia *his qualification was his disease* and that without this qualification the speech would have little impact. Because of this, he made sure that the audience knew. This is the way he began his speech:

be believable

109

I am a hemophiliac. To many of you, that word signifies little or nothing. A few may pause a moment and then remember that it has something to do with bleeding. Probably none of you can appreciate the gigantic impact of what those words mean to me. . . .

What does it really mean to be a hemophiliac? The first indication comes in early childhood when a small scratch may bleed for hours. By the time the hemophiliac reaches school age, he begins to suffer from internal bleeding into muscles, joints, the stomach, the kidneys. This latter type is far more serious, for external wounds can usually be stopped in minutes with topical thromboplastin or a pressure bandage. But internal bleeding can be checked only by changes in the blood by means of transfusion or plasma injections. If internal bleeding into a muscle or joint goes unchecked repeatedly, muscle contraction and bone deformity inevitably result. My crooked left arm, the built-up heel on my right shoe, and the full-length brace on my left leg offer mute but undeniable testimony to that fact. Vocal evidence you hear; weak tongue muscles are likely to produce defective L and R sounds. . . .

My memories of childhood and adolescence are memories of pain and heartbreak. I remember missing school for weeks and months at a stretch—of being very proud because I attended school once for four whole weeks without missing a single day. I remember the three long years that I couldn't even walk because repeated hemorrhages had twisted my ankles and knees to pretzel-like forms. I remember being pulled to school in a wagon while other boys rode their bikes, and being pushed to my table. I remember sitting in the dark empty classroom by myself during recess while the others went out in the sun to run and play. And I remember the first terrible day at the big high school when I came on crutches and built-up shoes carrying my books in a sack around my neck.[14]

[14] From "Mingled Blood," a speech by Ralph Zimmermann, reprinted in full in *Contemporary American Speeches*, 2nd ed., eds. Wil A. Linkugel, R. R. Allen, and Richard L. Johannesen (Belmont, Calif.: Wadsworth Publishing Co., 1969), pp. 199–203. Reprinted by permission from *Winning Orations, 1956* (Evanston, Ill.: The Interstate Oratorical Association, 1956).

After seeing and hearing Ralph Zimmermann, no one could doubt for a moment that on the subject of hemophilia he knew what he was talking about.

As the examples of Ralph Zimmermann and the Army major so clearly illustrate, if an audience is to hold an image of a speaker as one worthy of being believed, they need to know his qualifications.

speak with candor

Candor, as *Webster's New World Dictionary* notes, implies two qualities—fairness and frankness.

Earlier in the chapter we used a story of Senator Edmund Muskie inviting a heckler to speak to illustrate how a speaker, by identifying himself with his audience's values, can improve his personal image. This story, however, also makes an important point about the relationship of fairness to believability.

A common feeling of our time is that if a person is confident of the rightness of his position he will have no objection to having all sides of an issue openly expressed. Conversely, we tend to feel that if one objects to having all sides represented he must have something to hide. Thus, when Senator Muskie told his hecklers he would like a chance to speak, and one of them responded: "You have a chance, we don't!" the senator was faced with what could have been a dangerous challenge to his believability. Here's how Mr. Muskie turned the challenge to his advantage:

> The senator leaned forward and said he would let the students send a representative to the podium to speak for them. "I'll give him 10 minutes of uninterrupted attention," Muskie said. "There is another side of this bargain, if on your part—and you listen to this part of the bargain—you give me your uninterrupted attention."[15]

[15] *The Kansas City Times*, September 26, 1968, pp. 1A and 13A.

After Senator Muskie completed his half of the bargain and the heckler had spoken, the newspaper reported: "The Washington and Jefferson students, who had shouted, laughed and chanted earlier, listened attentively as Muskie returned to the microphone."[16]

Experimenters have discovered that speakers, when facing audiences opposed to their position, tend to be more effective persuaders if they are willing to acknowledge opposition arguments. This objective approach, the experimenters found, worked even better when dealing with more educated audiences.[17]

Frankness or honesty, as well as fairness, is a dimension of candor that can contribute substantially to a speaker's image of believability. As we discussed earlier in the book, we are living in an age that is becoming less and less tolerant of hypocrisy and indirection. This does not, of course, provide the speaker with a license to verbally abuse his listeners. Those who attempt this approach usually find that their credibility has suffered as a result. But it does suggest that we tend to admire a person who stands up for what he thinks is right, even if we don't agree with him.

Malcolm X, to revert to an earlier illustration, could have used his break with Black Muslim leader Elija Muhammad to establish greater commonality with his Cory Methodist Church audience. But he didn't! Instead he used this situation to establish his integrity at the very outset of his speech by explicitly acknowledging his non-Christian religion. Thus, immediately after stating his topic, "The Ballot or the Bullet," Malcolm announced:

Before we try to explain what is meant by the ballot or the bullet, I would like to clarify something concerning myself. I'm still a Muslim, my religion is still Islam. That's my

---

[16] *The Kansas City Times*, September 26, 1968, pp. 1A and 13A.
[17] Cohen, *Attitude Change*, pp. 3–4.

personal belief. . . . I myself am a minister, not a Christian minister, but a Muslim minister.[18]

Only after this candid statement of his belief—a belief that Malcolm recognized as different from that of most of his listeners—did he move on to establish his identity with his audience. His honesty, however, undoubtedly contributed to Malcolm's general image of believability with his audience.

We have no doubt that candor, when mitigated by an attitude of good will toward the audience, can lend substance to the speaker's image of believability. Nevertheless, we would be remiss if we didn't indicate quite clearly that the "bitter truth" can be a great alienator. There are times, as every sensitive observer of human behavior knows, when excessive frankness is neither desirable nor necessary. An incident reported in *This Week* magazine makes the point. Mister Karl, a music teacher in Atlanta, received the following note from the mother of one of his students: "I appreciate your comments about Stephen's musical ability but on your next report, we would rather you didn't give us your honest opinion."[19] Clearly, candor in public speaking is a two-edged sword that must be used with great care.

give good reasons

"Man," wrote philosopher Blaise Pascal, "is but a reed, the most feeble thing in nature, but he is a thinking reed." Even though man does not always act rationally he is proud of his rational nature. Rationality, therefore, constitutes the fourth category of message effectiveness in constituting an image of believability.

In speechmaking, rationality refers simply to the ability to give good reasons. Good reasons, in turn, are made up of two elements—*evidence* and *inference*. Evidence is the information

---

[18] *Malcolm X Speaks*, p. 24.

[19] Bill Adler, "Dear Music Teacher," *This Week*, March 9, 1969, p. 16.

we begin with, while inference is the way we use that information to reach conclusions. The following sections consider each in turn.

evidence

Although many different people have talked about the subject of evidence in many different ways, we feel that there is value in simplifying our discussion by dividing the topic into three major categories: *example, quantification,* and *testimony.*

Example   Discussing the sources of belief, the authors of a well-known book on debating stress the role played by experience:

> "Seeing is believing." "Show me." "Experience is the best teacher." "The tongue of experience has the most truth." These and similar adages emphasize the reliance traditionally placed on experience as a source of belief. Nor can it be denied that many beliefs are the direct result of what one has himself seen, tried, felt, or undergone.[20]

For the public speaker, the example is a means of symbolically constituting, or reconstituting, experience for his listeners. Thus, through the use of meaningful language, the skillful speaker is able to simulate to a large degree that concreteness which accounts for much of the impact of personal experience.[21]

If it is true, therefore, that personal experience is a basic source of belief, then the example, too, can become a basic source of belief. If firsthand knowledge of bloody, death-deal-

[20] Douglas Ehninger and Wayne Brockriede, *Decision by Debate* (New York: Dodd, Mead & Co., 1963), p. 194.

[21] The ideas concerning the prepotent position of the example as a means of inducting belief resulted, in part, from conversations with Professor Charles Ledbetter of Thornton Junior College, Harvey, Illinois.

ing automobile accidents will induce a person to drive more carefully, then vivid word pictures of bloody, death-dealing automobile accidents will promote the believability of that same proposition. If personal knowledge of the pain, fear, and death of a cancer ward will influence a person to stop smoking cigarettes, then an intense symbolic representation of that scene will impel him in the same direction.

In our minds, there is no question that the speaker who is able to discern those kinds of experiences that are, or could be, meaningful to his audience, and reproduce them symbolically through language, will add proportionately to his image of believability.

There are, obviously, different kinds of examples. Which will prove most useful in establishing believability will depend on the speaker's purpose and the situation in which it is directed. The following cases should prove useful in distinguishing the various uses of examples.

Miss Carolyn Kay Geiman, a former student at the University of Kansas, was intensely interested in the plight of the culturally deprived child. In a classroom speech on the subject, her goal was to establish the idea that these children "are not innately unintelligent, and this deficiency [cultural deprivation] can and should be corrected." She goes on to demonstrate, through the use of example, how an experimental program was able to overcome a lack of language development:

Rhoda was one of the subjects of this experiment. In the classroom she stands, "clutching her favorite toys—a Negro doll and a toy baby bottle. The only game she knows is caring for the baby—bathing it, feeding it, rocking it. Fatherless Rhoda lives with her mother, who bore her at fifteen, her thirty-eight year old grandmother, two younger sisters, and eight uncles and aunts ranging in age from two months to ten years. After eleven weeks in school, Rhoda still hasn't spoken or smiled. Scowling fiercely now, she reaches out for some wax grapes and puts them in a frying pan on the stove." Hearing a noise behind her, the teacher turned around to discover Rhoda struggling with a pan. She heard Rhoda speak her first whole sentence: "Dem goddam peaches is burnin'." It's poor English, it's profane, but it is a complete thought, and this is a major achievement. Rhoda was rewarded with a big hug from her teacher, not scolded for her profanity.

Projects such as this one indicate that with care, understanding, and attention children in slum areas can be helped in mastering the basic skill of communication so vital to their educational process.[22]

In this instance, the speaker used what we might call a real example—something that actually happened. Although Miss Geiman found the materials for her example in a published report, the speaker's personal experience, when appropriate, can also be a fruitful source of such evidence. Ralph Zimmermann, in a speech we cited earlier, refers to himself as an example that a hemophiliac can improve:

Once a hemophiliac successfully passes through the dangerous period, his need for blood steadily decreases and his health improves. The nightmare of youth is gradually hidden behind a protective curtain of objectivity that is seldom raised. In contrast to my childhood days, I can look back on more than three years of college with joy and a sense of achievement. I've had some good breaks. I've been in debate and forensics for four years and had a variety of satisfying experiences. I've been lucky in politics. My constituents, the student body at our college, elected me President of Student Government. Like so many other American youths, I've worked my way through college as a clerk in a hardware store. On warm weekends, while not a Ben Hogan at golf, I have shot an 82. And back home, a girl wears my wedding band.[23]

[22] From "Are They Really 'Unteachable'?" a speech by Carolyn Kay Geiman, reprinted in full in Linkugel, Allen, and Johannesen, 2nd ed., pp. 94–98. Reprinted by permission of Miss Geiman.

[23] Speech by Zimmermann; see footnote 14.

No matter how effective a real example can be, a speaker will find occasionally that none will make the point with which he is concerned. In such cases, he may choose to invent a hypothetical example. The invented example, if it is to be effective, however, must not depart from the essence of reality. In other words, the real world may be expanded or compressed, but the circumstances which go to make up the hypothetical example must be consistent with listeners' views of reality.

In a speech on business ethics, David Fromson found that a hypothetical example (in this case, a composite of real situations) suited his purpose better than any real example could have. To make his point that there is a lack of ethics in business, Fromson describes a day in the life of Mr. Executive:

As he walks to his down town office, after leaving his car resting smugly in a No Parking zone, he warmly greets the veteran cop on the beat, who thanks him for his recent annual present, a case of good blended whiskey (penalty for attempting to influence a police officer with a gift: $5,000 fine and/or ten years in jail). After a few routine desk chores the businessman has a profitable late morning session with his personal income tax consultant, who has found a happy device for distorting repair and depreciation costs on some rental property he owns (penalty for filing a fraudulent income tax return: $10,000 fine and/or five years in jail). By this time he has worked up an appetite for a good expense account meal, so he entertains his wife and two close friends at a lavish lunch, all on company tab (a misdemeanor under section 665 of the State Penal Law subject to a $500 fine and/or one year in jail). Back in the office, he reminds one of his assistants to "take care of" the building inspector with jurisdiction over their new plant site, thus getting as much red tape out of the way as possible (penalty for bribing public officers: $5,000 fine and/or ten years in jail). He then dictates a letter to an executive of a small concern with which he has just signed a contract thanking him for his thoughtful gift of a new model portable TV set (penalty for secretly accepting a gift in return for corporate favors: $500 fine and/or one year in jail).[24]

As his work day closes, Mr. Executive carries on.

[He] asks his secretary to wrap up one of the new company desk sets, which will be just the thing for his den at home (penalty for appropriating company property to one's personal use: $500 fine and/or one year in jail). Safe at home, he advises his wife not to worry about the maid's social security payments because she is leaving soon anyway (penalty for willful nonpayment of employer's social security contributions: $10,000 fine and/or five years in jail). Laying aside the cares of the day, he settles down to watch the news on his souvenir TV set—and fulminates about the dishonesty of the union racketeers he sees on the screen.[25]

The speaker, in using this hypothetical example, was able to demonstrate the ethical and legal significance of a number of common practices in the business world. Singly, the practices appear of little consequence and are easy to rationalize. Seen in mass, however, the scope of the problem becomes clear. To achieve this end required that Mr. Fromson create a hypothetical person, Mr. Executive. For his particular purposes, this device was more effective in establishing the believability of his proposition than a real example would have been.

In an analogy, one situation (example) which is better understood by the audience or which is more vivid or more memorable is used as the basis for conclusions about a second situation which is less well known or less vivid or memorable.

Advertising executive Bruce Barton, for illustration, turned to an analogy in his famous speech, "Which Knew Not Joseph," when he wanted to impress upon a group of public relations men that they must continue their efforts every day.

[24] David Fromson, "Business Ethics, Your Trade Association, and the Invisible Hand," *Vital Speeches of the Day*, Vol. 32 (October 15, 1965), p. 29. Reprinted by special permission.

[25] Fromson, p. 29.

The account of Joseph in the Old Testament . . . tells how he left his country under difficulties and, coming into a strange country, he arose through his diligence, to become the principal person in the state, second only to the King. Now, gentlemen, the Biblical narrative brings us to that point—the point where Joseph had public relations with all the other ancient nations, while his private relations held all the best-paying jobs—it brings us up to the climax of his career and then it hands us an awful jolt. Without any words of preparation or explanation, it says bluntly:

"And Joseph died, and there arose a new king in Egypt which knew not Joseph."

I submit, gentlemen, that this is one of the most staggering lines which has ever been written in a business biography. Here was a man so famous that everybody knew him and presto, a few people die, a few new ones are born, and *nobody* knows him. The tide of human life has moved on; the king who exalted the friends of Joseph is followed by a king who makes them slaves; all the advertising that the name "Joseph" had enjoyed in one generation is futile and of no avail, because that generation has gone.

Now, what has all that to do with you? Very much indeed. When we gathered in this room this afternoon, there were in this country, in bed, sick, several thousand old men. It perhaps is indelicate for me to refer to that fact, but it is a fact, and we are grown up and we have to face these things. On those old men you gentlemen collectively have spent a considerable amount of time and a considerable amount of money. It is to be supposed that you have made some impression upon them regarding your service and your purposes and your necessities. But in this interval, while we have been sitting here, those old men have died and all your time and all your money and whatever you have built up in the way of good will in their minds—*all* your labor and investment have passed out with them.

In the same brief interval, there have been born in this country, several thousand lusty boys and girls to whom you gentlemen mean no more than the Einstein theory. They do not know the difference between a Mazda Lamp and a stick of Wrigley's chewing gum. Nobody has ever told them that Ivory

Soap floats or that children cry for Castoria, or what sort of soap you ought to use if you want to have a skin that people would like to touch. The whole job of giving them the information they are going to need in order to form an intelligent public opinion and to exercise an intelligent influence in the community has to be started from the beginning and done over again.

So the first very simple thing that I would say to you (and it is so simple that it seems to me it ought to be said at every convention of this kind) is that this business of public relations is a very constant business, that the fact that you told your story yesterday should not lead you into the delusion of supposing that you have ever told it. . . .

Cultivating good will is a day-by-day and hour-by-hour business, gentlemen. Every day and every hour the "king" dies and there arises a new "king" to whom you and all your works mean absolutely nothing.[26]

This story of the rise and fall of the biblical Joseph may, at first glance, appear to be just another example. Mr. Barton, however, is not concerned about Bible history—at least not in this speech. What he is concerned about is making believable the idea that public relations men must be constantly on guard or they will lose their gains. He uses an illustration from the Bible simply because by so doing he is able to give dramatic impact to a rather ordinary idea. Mr. Barton's assumption—and the assumption underlying all analogy—is that if the audience can be induced to accept a conclusion about one situation, it will be more likely to accept the same conclusion about a similar or related circumstance.

Billy Graham, in the excerpt of his speech cited in Chapter 2, makes a similar use of analogy. In that instance, Graham told of a situation where labor leader Walter Reuther was accepted by a hostile audience because of his sincerity. Although Graham never makes the comparison explicit, his point

[26] From Robert T. Oliver and Rupert L. Cortright, *New Training for Effective Speech*, rev. ed. (New York: Dryden Press, 1951), pp. 123–124.

is clear to all—"if a group of industrialists will accept Walter Reuther for his honesty, you should accept me for mine."

Analogies, of course, can be based on relationships that are figurative, as well as on those that are literal. Russell Conwell, for instance, became famous toward the end of the last century by presenting his speech "Acres of Diamonds" on lecture tours throughout the country. In this speech Conwell tells the story of a man who sold his farm and spent the rest of his life searching for diamonds, only to have the purchaser of the farm find them in the back yard. Conwell then asserts that each of us has acres of diamonds in our own back yards in the sense that we all have many opportunities:

> I say to you that you have "acres of diamonds" in Philadelphia right where you now live. "Oh," but you will say, "you cannot know much about your city if you think there are any 'acres of diamonds' here." . . .
>
> But it serves simply to illustrate my thought, which I emphasize by saying if you do not have the actual diamond-mines literally you have all that they would be good for to you.[27]

Acres of diamonds and unlimited opportunity are not, of course, literally the same. Conwell, however, uses the example of diamonds, which we all recognize as valuable, to help his audience recognize the less obvious, but equal, value of every-day opportunities.

Examples, because of their ability to reproduce experience, are one of the foremost tools available to the speaker concerned with the problem of believability.

Quantification   In a society that holds science in such high esteem it is understandable that the public will tend to find believable those data (a "scientific" term for information) that are presented as precise quantities. Quantification, which is

---

[27] From Ernest J. Wrage and Barnet Baskerville, eds., *American Forum: Speeches on Historic Issues, 1788–1900* (New York: Harper & Row, 1960), pp. 269–270.

essentially describing through numbers, can have two applications in public speaking. The first is as a means of characterizing a single entity, while the second provides a method of comparing one instance with many similar instances.

A speech written by the public relations staff of the Bell Telephone System to tell of its Telstar Satellite illustrates the first application of quantification in a public speech:

> On July 10, 1962, at 4:35 A.M., a Delta rocket blazed off pad 17 at Cape Canaveral carrying the Bell System's Telstar Satellite. It was a "shot heard around the world!"...
>
> Telstar comes in a small package like so many other amazing devices in our miniaturized wonder world of electronics. This little sphere of aluminum and magnesium is 34½ inches in diameter—only slightly larger than a beach ball. But it's worth more than its weight in gold. Four hundred Bell Telephone Laboratories scientists, engineers and technicians worked on the development of Telstar and associated microwave experiments. More than 15,000 components had to be put together, inspected and tested before it could be boosted into the blue.[28]

Neither our image of the intricacy of Telstar nor our image of the knowledgeableness of the speaker would have been nearly so well developed without the use of quantification. Through the use of figures, the speaker was able to describe both the precise time and place of Telstar's launch, as well as the details of the satellite itself.

The second application of quantification to speaking is commonly referred to as statistics. Although we may not often think of them in this way, statistical data are really nothing more than quantification of the same kinds of information from which examples are drawn. When statistics are used as

[28] From "Telstar," a speech by members of the public relations staff of the American Telephone and Telegraph Company, reprinted in full in *Contemporary American Speeches*, eds. Wil A. Linkugel, R. R. Allen, and Richard L. Johannesen (Belmont, Calif.: Wadsworth Publishing Co., 1965), pp. 45–51. Reprinted by permission of the Bell System.

evidence in a speech, their function is to provide a workable way of presenting information of what might otherwise be thought of as a large number of examples. Whereas an example depicts a given phenomenon concretely, a statistic indicates in abstract terms how it relates to other phenomena. Is it, for instance, similar to or different from others? Are there many cases, or is it a limited occurrence?

In a speech on world population increase, Daniel Crary uses statistical information to demonstrate the seriousness of the problem:

It has been estimated that at the beginning of the Christian era the population of the world was something like 300 million. Today, 1,960 years later, the world population is estimated just at three billion, ten times greater than it was in New Testament days. But the best conservative information, which is now available from United Nations demographers, says flatly that this increase in population, which has taken us nearly 2,000 years, is going to be *repeated*, not in 2,000 years, but in 40. The 1958 publication *Future Growth of World Population* from the U.N. states that the population of the world by 2000 A.D. will be seven billion.[29]

Later, Mr. Crary combines example and statistic in order to demonstrate both the nature of the overpopulation problem and its extensiveness:

The country of Brazil is developing economically but can barely keep up with the rise in population. In India, population increases *every year* by the total population of Canada! Egypt's Aswan Dam, which was to spur Egypt to greater economic heights, will soon be completed, but when it is, Egypt's economy will be behind what it was before the construction began, because population has grown faster than the benefits of the project. According to statistics of the United

[29] From "A Plague of People," a speech by Daniel R. Crary, reprinted in full in Linkugel, Allen, and Johannesen, 2nd ed. (1969), pp. 220–224. Reprinted by permission of Mr. Crary.

Nations and the International Monetary Fund, these examples are typical of 70 to 80 percent of all less developed countries. Instead of advancing economically, in terms of population growth and internal problems they are stagnating or regressing.[30]

The coordinated use of examples and statistics has obvious advantages in the development of believable messages. An example may be effective in showing people as flesh and blood, but the listener is likely to respond: "Your example is interesting, but is it typical? Is the problem widespread enough to worry about?" On the other hand, statistics may demonstrate that an instance is typical or that a problem is extensive, but they are often dull and lifeless. With examples and statistics in combination, however, the speaker is capable of presenting a more complete, and therefore more believable, picture.

Summarizing, quantification is valuable to the speaker in that it provides him with a means of describing precisely the nature of some entity as well as a method for showing its relationship to others in its class. Furthermore, by using quantification the speaker provides evidence of his expertise—his ability to deal with his subject "scientifically."

Testimony   Testimony is sometimes referred to as authority evidence, but such terminology may be misleading. Not all testimony is authoritative. Consider, for example, a well-known actress who endorses a chain of car transmission repair shops or the professional quarterback who asserts the superiority of a particular brand of electric razor while shaving off his famous mustache. Is the actress an expert on car transmissions? Is the quarterback an authority on electric razors? In each case, the answer is very likely No.

Although people such as film stars and professional athletes may be celebrities, they are ordinarily no more qualified to testify on behalf of the products they endorse than anyone else. Intelligent audiences are well aware of this fact. The astute

[30] Speech by Crary; see footnote 29.

speaker, therefore, will usually not turn to these sources of testimony.

To be believable, the person testifying, like the speaker himself, must be recognized as qualified. If the expert cited by the speaker is not recognized by the audience, his credential must be established by the speaker if the testimony is to be meaningful. This suggests that a speaker is well advised, when possible, to search out authorities who are already known and respected by the audience he is addressing.

Adlai Stevenson, a man who was known as a brilliant public speaker, illustrates the use of testimony by men who, for most audiences, would require no qualification. In a speech at the University of California at Berkeley, while he was ambassador to the United Nations, Stevenson argued in favor of a policy of internationalism:

> It was King Solomon who said, "Knowledge is a wonderful thing; therefore get knowledge; but with all thy getting, get understanding."
>
> I could suggest no harder task, no greater challenge to a university in our complex world. . . . It is the aspiration of the university to make free men wise.
>
> Thomas Jefferson proclaimed that the United States was the strongest nation on earth not because of its military might or its productive capacity, but because of its revolutionary ideas. The American Revolution, he said, is intended for all mankind. And I would remind you that there would have been no American Revolution had we not had men who were free and wise and, therefore, not afraid to stand up and rock the boat.[31]

In an address to the Annual Leadership Conference of the Arkansas Federation of Business and Professional Women's Clubs, Ralph Eubanks inauspiciously but effectively qualifies

[31] From " 'Let Us Work While It Is Yet Day,' " a speech by Adlai E. Stevenson, reprinted in full in Linkugel, Allen, and Johannesen (1965), pp. 286–294. Reprinted by permission from a pamphlet by the World Law Fund, 11 West 42nd Street, New York, N.Y.

his use of authority. Eubanks, a professor of speech, recognized that his audience would probably not know some of the experts he cites in his keynote address, "Leadership and the 'Sane Society.'"

> We must aspire to a sound public philosophy based on the order of persons; which is to say, upon matters spiritual instead of matters mechanical. For a general guide, I can think of no better than that offered by Bertram Morris, the American philosopher, in his recent book, *Philosophical Aspects of Culture*. Morris holds that movement from a "less genuine to a more genuine culture," is measured in terms of "the achievement of ends and the care for persons in the process. Without achievement of ends [Morris explains] a society is impotent, and without caring for persons, achievement is suicidal.". . .
>
> The ideal modern leader must therefore be more than a clear thinker in the technical matters of positive science and technology. . . . Jacques Barzun—a modern scholar whose writings have profoundly affected my life—puts the point well. "Intellect," says Barzun, "belongs largely to the Western tradition—the tradition of explicitness and energy, of inquiry and debate. . . . What Intellect satisfies in us is the need for orderly and perspicuous expression, which may lead to common belief and concerted action."[32]

A quality other than expertise which often contributes to the believability of testimony is that associated with what has been termed the "reluctant witness." If a person has a vested interest in the proposition he is supporting, his testimony may be suspect regardless of his other qualifications. In contrast, the man who appears to be testifying in opposition to his own best interest has a special element of believability. This knowledge was applied by Anthony Arpaia in his speech, "A Matter of Necessity." In advocating a system of binding arbitration in labor disputes—a position generally opposed by labor unions

---

[32] From "Leadership and the 'Sane Society,'" a speech by Ralph T. Eubanks, reprinted in full in Linkugel, Allen, and Johannesen (1965), pp. 178–186. Reprinted by special permission from *Vital Speeches of the Day* (May 15, 1963), pp. 478–480.

—Mr. Arpaia cites witness of David McDonald, at that time president of the United Steelworkers union:

> Irresponsibility, even in a free society, has its limitations. As David J. McDonald of the United Steelworkers said in a recent speech, "We must perform our roles as Americans concerned first with the common good." A better way than tests of raw economic force must be found to resolve labor-management issues when collective bargaining fails.[33]

Finally, testimony may be used, not for its authoritativeness, but for the effectiveness of its expression. Thus, in a speech condemning contemporary penal institutions, an ex-convict says:

> During my three hundred and forty-six days as an inmate I saw many things. I met men I never knew existed before. My dorm mates were murderers, rapists, and dope addicts. You name them and I dormed with them. I had the opportunity to talk with them and to hear the very twisted thoughts which they had. . . .
> Oscar Wilde put it this way in his poem entitled "Ballad of Reading Gaol":
>> The Vilest deeds like poison weeds,
>> Bloom well in prison air,
>> It is only what is good in Man
>> That wastes and withers there.[34]

Testimony, like examples and quantification, can become convincing evidence. To cite an authority of our own—the authors of a book entitled *Thinking and Speaking:* "Quotations are useful because they give the weight of authority to an

[33] From "A Matter of Necessity," a speech by Anthony F. Arpaia, reprinted in full in Linkugel, Allen, and Johannesen (1965), pp. 240–250. Reprinted by special permission from *Vital Speeches of the Day* (May 15, 1964), pp. 477–480.

[34] From "Man's Other Society," a speech by Richard M. Duesterbeck, reprinted in full in Linkugel, Allen, and Johannesen (1965), pp. 264–268. Reprinted by permission from *Winning Orations, 1961* (Evanston, Ill.: The Interstate Oratorical Association, 1961), pp. 100–102.

opinion (which accounts for the myriad times George Washington's advice 'to avoid entangling foreign alliances' has been quoted by American politicians) or because they phrase an idea in a particularly striking manner (which accounts for the frequent use of Shakespeare's words) or both (which accounts for the frequent use of that most quoted book, the Bible)."[35]

drawing conclusions from evidence

During a recent social gathering with several colleagues and their wives, our conversation turned first to travel, then to New York City, and, finally, to New York taxi drivers. The discussion went something like this:

First Colleague The distance from the restaurant back to our hotel wasn't far, but we were in a hurry so we took a cab. I paid the fare, which was less than a dollar, and gave the driver a quarter tip—something like 30 percent of the tab. We had taken only a few steps toward the hotel when we heard this commotion behind us and turned to see what it was. Our cab driver was standing there, pointing to the quarter in his outstretched hand and shouting obscenities. Then he threw the quarter at our feet and got back in his cab.

Second Colleague Something similar once happened to me in New York. Several of us got together and took a taxi out to the airport. Cab drivers in New York hate long trips because it cuts down on their tips, so our driver wasn't in too good a mood to begin with. When we finally got to the airport, one of our group decided to pay the bill and then collect from the rest later. Knowing the tipping habits of the person, I sensed that there might be a scene; so I grabbed my suitcase and moved out as fast as I could. It wasn't fast enough, however; in the background I could hear the driver cursing loudly over what he considered the insufficiency of his tip. New York cab drivers must be the world's surliest group.

[35] Otis M. Walter and Robert L. Scott, *Thinking and Speaking: A Guide to Intelligent Oral Communication* (New York: Macmillan Co., 1962), p. 45.

Third Colleague I don't agree with that at all. The last time I was in New York my cab drivers were talkative, friendly, and helpful. I didn't tip them excessively, but they seemed appreciative.

In this conversation, no one doubted the experiences that the others had, but there was genuine disagreement over the conclusions drawn from those experiences. The experiences in this case we can call evidence, which is what we have just been discussing. Evidence, of course, is an important part of the process of rationality, which, in turn, bears heavily on the development of the believable images sought by public speakers.

As our discussion of New York cab drivers indicates, however, evidence in itself is not enough to guarantee a particular conclusion. The process which leads from evidence to conclusion is called *inference*. Making inferences is, of course, a necessary part of every person's life. But most of us have probably never given much thought to the process itself. Yet, if we are to be successful in drawing believable conclusions from evidence, we must understand something about how the inference process works.

The basic elements of proof The combination of evidence, inference, and conclusion is generally referred to as proof. A Scottish logician, Stephen Toulmin, has developed a theory of proof which public speakers have discovered to be extremely useful in understanding how the process works.[36]

According to Toulmin's theory, there are three basic elements of proof. Although our terminology is different than that employed by Toulmin, the three elements are essentially those we have identified as evidence, inference, and conclusion. The relationship of these elements, as Toulmin views it, is indicated in the following diagram:

[36] Stephen Toulmin, *Uses of Argument* (Cambridge, England: Cambridge University Press, 1958).

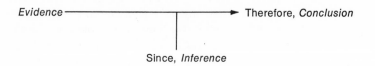

Evidence ────────────────► Therefore, *Conclusion*

Since, *Inference*

If we apply this model to the conversation with which we opened our discussion of inference, the diagram looks like this:

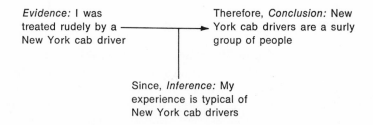

Evidence: I was treated rudely by a New York cab driver ────────► Therefore, *Conclusion:* New York cab drivers are a surly group of people

Since, *Inference:* My experience is typical of New York cab drivers

Usually, we tend not to make the basis of our inferences explicit. When we do, as in the above diagram, it becomes embarrassingly clear that we have been engaging in some pretty shoddy reasoning. It's little wonder that our colleague who had had a different experience was unwilling to accept our conclusions about the surliness of New York cab drivers as a group.

The secondary elements of proof   Evidence, inference, and conclusion, as we have discussed them, constitute the basic elements of proof. Although it is true that the proof cannot exist if any one of the three is missing, it is also clear that the mere existence of the three elements does not necessarily make the proof believable.

Thus, the Toulmin model includes three secondary elements: *Backing for the inference, reservations,* and a *qualifier.* These secondary elements are required to make proof acceptable to most audiences in all but the simplest situations.

By backing for the inference we mean that inferences, like the original conclusion, will often require evidence of their own. In the case of our example, most people could be expected to ask how we know that our experience was typical. If we answer that question honestly, we will have to admit that the only backing we have for our inference is a couple of similar experiences we remember hearing about. Even then, if pushed, we would have to concede that we can't recall anything specific about the examples—who told us, when the incidents took place, and so forth.

Once we have begun to dissect our original contention about New York cab drivers on the basis of the Toulmin model, the inadequacy of our reasoning becomes even more evident. A person would have to be a fool to accept conclusions based on such insufficient evidence and reasoning. In fact, one could conclude that only a fool would expect anyone to accept this kind of proof. Yet, sadly enough, intelligent and well-educated people often think in ways that are equally inadequate.

What, we might ask, can be done to make our argument concerning New York cab drivers more believable? A different kind of backing for our inference, you'll probably agree, would help considerably. Suppose, for example, we could say that we have lived in New York City for ten years, ridden in its taxis frequently, and can attest to the fact that the example we have used is typical. If our colleague who had the pleasant experience with taxi drivers in New York was only an occasional visitor to the city, he would probably defer to our greater experience and thus accept our conclusion.

Of course, if one cannot provide backing for his inference from personal experience, he may be able to find some authority who will testify to the fact. As you have probably already noted, everything we wrote earlier about evidence in general is applicable to the problem of providing backing for inferences.

In addition to backing for inferences, proof patterns, to be believable, may also require reservations or a qualifier. A reservation is simply an acknowledgment that under certain circumstances there may be exceptions to the evidence-inference-conclusion pattern that has been established. We may have to concede, for example, that if one tips excessively or that if the driver is in a good mood, our conclusions about New York cabbies may not be true.

A qualifier is a way of including in our proof the admission that very few things in this world are absolute. It simply incorporates into our reasoning process the idea contained in the old adage that nothing is certain except death and taxes. As Douglas Ehninger and Wayne Brockriede put it:

> The need to qualify claim statements [conclusions] stems from either or both of two sources. If the evidence or warrant [inference] is in any way qualified, then the claim [conclusion] should have corresponding qualification, by such terms as "possibly," "probably," "at the 5 percent level of confidence," "almost certainly," and others. A second need for qualification arises when the claim [conclusion] is accepted only under the condition that reservations can be cancelled out. Until one has satisfactorily disposed of the doubt cast by the reservations, he must qualify his claim [conclusion] with "presumably," "probably," or a similar term.[37]

Diagramed, complete with backing for inference, reservations, and qualifier, our original argument would look like this:

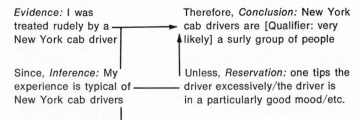

Evidence: I was treated rudely by a New York cab driver

Therefore, Conclusion: New York cab drivers are [Qualifier: very likely] a surly group of people

Since, Inference: My experience is typical of New York cab drivers

Unless, Reservation: one tips the driver excessively/the driver is in a particularly good mood/etc.

Because, Backing for Inference: Sociologist X conducted a survey which found that 80% of the time New York cab drivers are abusive to their customers

[37] Ehninger and Brockriede, *Decision by Debate*, pp. 106–107.

If we had presented this kind of argument in the first place, our colleague who got the friendly driver would probably have been willing to accept our conclusion. There can be little doubt that, most of the time, if our inferences are to result in believable messages, they must be given appropriate backing, reservation, and qualification.

RELEVANT CLEAR

SPEAKER

BELIEVABLE INTERESTING

6

let's put it together

Benjamin Disraeli once observed, "It is much easier to be critical than to be correct." Thus warned, we propose in this chapter to take a look at a completed speech, to explicate its strategy and design, and to evaluate it critically in terms of the concepts we have elaborated in previous chapters. We will discuss the choices the speaker made in terms of his listeners, whether they be good or bad, and will examine which rhetorical tools he chose to apply in his speech. We hope, by taking the reader through the makeup of an actual speech, that we can bring into sharp focus the rhetorical concepts of this book, and, thereby, help the reader himself prepare better addresses. We may not be critical at every point, nor may we always be correct, but we do hope to be instructional throughout.

The speech you are about to read was given by a college sophomore in a college speech class. It was delivered extemporaneously with the aid of a few note cards. We tape-recorded it and have reproduced it here in manuscript form. The speaker, Ernie Link, came from a small western Kansas town. He was a somewhat better than average student, but was not one of the most prominent members of his speech class. He spoke in a quiet but sincere and earnest tone of voice. His concern for his subject seemed genuine.

The class audience numbered twenty-three: fifteen freshmen, five sophomores, and three upper classmen. The listeners represented a cross section of liberal arts and science college students. Since the audience had no advance notice of the topic or the speaker's qualifications to speak on that topic, Ernie

Link had to rely on the speech itself to attract the audience's interest and to establish the relevance of his topic.

The title of the speech is "Come Take My Hand." The text of the speech is in the left-hand column. In the right-hand column we have written our comments concerning that portion of the speech. Before you read our comments, you may want to read the speech in its entirety in order to get a total perspective of it.

1 I was raised in a small Midwestern town and when I say small I mean *small*. The streets there were unpaved and quite dusty. In the summer the scorching sun powdered the dust, and the hot southern winds scattered the dust everywhere, coating the grass and the tree leaves until they were no longer green. They would become a shabby brown. The grass would release billows of dust when you walked through it. My family was lucky; we could afford to water our lawn and wash part of the dust off our grass, revealing that pleasing green color. The family across the street from us was not so fortunate. They could not afford to water their lawn and there was only a little grass on it. Their lawn was smaller than ours, and it was mostly hot, exposed, packed earth.

2 Sometimes I would walk by and see a red toy tractor lying on one of the patches of grass. It had only one wheel. The lawn

Public speakers commonly try to identify with their audiences at the outset of their speeches. This may include appropriate references to the occasion, the locale, or past relationships; often humor is used for this purpose. Sometimes a significant portion of the speech is devoted to this end. Theodore Roosevelt, one of the most prominent public speakers our nation has produced, sometimes got so wound up with occasional matters that it was a struggle for him to get to his theme. Ernie Link, by contrast, begins his speech by moving directly to his subject. He apparently assumes an identity or rapport with his audience at the outset. Perhaps this is valid thinking since in a speech class, unlike in most social situations, a person at one moment is the speaker but the next he is a member of the listening audience. It may also be that in other situations it is appropriate to observe certain social amenities at the outset of stretched out in front of their four-room frame house. I had heard that three of the rooms were bedrooms. This was probably true; after all, there were six children in the family. There used to be seven but one of the girls died. Tommy, my age, was the oldest of their children. He came to school the first day with his hair cut and he was wearing a clean shirt and a tie. The tie seemed kind of out of place—none of the other first-graders had on ties. His large baggy pants also seemed alien.

3   In the first grade almost everyone talked a lot, but Tommy didn't talk much the first day. Nor did he talk much the second day either. Sometimes our teacher would ask Tommy questions, but he would never answer them. He only shook his head and looked down at the top of his small, wooden desk. Tommy was different; he didn't speak well, and he couldn't express his thoughts to others. He never had the opportunity nor incentive to talk. He was one of those economically and socially deprived children that we hear so much about today.

the speech, but as often as not they could be dispensed with.

The critical question concerning Ernie Link's opening paragraph is whether it establishes needed rapport with his audience and whether it enlists their interest in hearing what he has to say. To this end, he begins with a personal anecdote. The story he narrates involves a specific person, a disadvantaged boy named Tommy, and it makes good use of mental imagery. Both are strong interest factors. The story also identifies the speaker with the subject he is going to talk about. It springs from his personal experience. There is a chance, however, that some listeners might find the story misleading, for not until the very end does the speaker indicate what he is leading up to. In fact, there is every reason to believe that the speech will be about dust storms or soil conservation, perhaps even home beautification.

How do you react to Ernie Link's opening story? Do you find it interesting? Believable? Appropriate to his subject? Relevant to the audience he is addressing? Do you find it in any way embarrassing to you?

We invite you to compare Ernie Link's opening with a different opening paragraph that we have taken from another student's speech on virtually the same subject.

let's put it together

Within the big doughnut-shaped arena encircling the central complex of major cities reside the poverty-stricken slum dwellers. Many are newcomers, fleeing from frustrations of life in the deep South and Appalachia to the bewilderment of the city slum, searching for elusive advantages which never come to pass. Tomorrow, they say, they will return to the farm; history says they are here to stay. Some are attempting to build their second or third set of hopes; to others, time has taught the futility of dreams, aspirations, and initiative. But what about their children's aspirations? Do they have a chance for a better life?

This introduction has the advantage of disclosing the general subject of the speech in the very first sentence. It also gets to the subject much quicker. On the other hand, it has less interest value and no personal involvement.

Which approach to beginning the speech do you like better, this one or Ernie Link's story about Tommy? One might choose still other ways of beginning the speech—with startling statements, with statistics, with a quotation, or with reference to a news event. Later in our critical comments we will suggest another possibility for an introduction. If you do not like either of the openings thus far presented, how do you feel the speech on Head Start could most appropriately be introduced?

4 Gowen and Demos in their book *The Disadvantaged and Potential Dropout* report that in 1950 one out of every ten children in the United States' fourteen largest cities was considered as being disadvantaged. By 1960 the figure rose to one out of three, and by 1970 it is estimated that one out of every two urban children will be disadvantaged. According to George W. Jones, field representative for the National Education Association Urban Services Division, there are over fourteen and one half million disadvantaged youngsters under seventeen in this country today.

In Paragraph 4, Ernie Link moves from his opening story to a general view of the scope of the problem that Tommy represents. He thus moves from a specific example—Tommy—to the general problem—expressed through statistics. He identifies the sources of his statistics and tries to make them meaningful by expressing them in different units. He first uses a chronological approach, citing by decade how the numbers of disadvantaged have increased; then he gives the collective total of disadvantaged; finally he relates the figure "fourteen and a half million" to other units of

Fourteen and one half million: Fourteen and one half million people would make 966 schools the size of K.U. at the present time. It would make seven states with the population that Kansas now has, or would be as large as the entire state of California at the present time.

5 Perhaps you are wondering what I have in mind when I speak of disadvantaged children. Exactly what is a disadvantaged child? Is he a child who lives in an urban slum area, a child who has a number of siblings and only a mother to support them? Is he a child who lives in the hills of Kentucky or Tennessee and has never seen a city, a zoo, a museum, even a train or a bus? Is he a child who lives in a rural area of New England and attends a one-room school with children from grades one through eight, a child who has never walked in a park or ridden on a bus, who has been no farther than his grandparents' house 40 miles away? Disadvantaged children could be any of these things, but the one common element is that they are the victims of social and economic misfortune. They are affected by environmental factors that limit their aspirations and achievements. William E. Amos, Chief of

measurement that allow the audience to visualize its magnitude more readily, using the University of Kansas, the state of Kansas, and the state of California as his comparative agents. This paragraph serves the vital function of impressing upon the listener that Tommy is not an isolated example and that the problem indeed is of consequence. We think that his technique in this paragraph is effective.

Paragraph 5 defines a "disadvantaged child." The speaker's technique again is interesting. He asks three rhetorical questions which embody possible definitions and then he supplies a definition that may encompass all of those factors. The questions serve the purpose of helping the listener visualize the nature and scope of the deprivation being discussed. Amos's definition alone is in the abstract. The speaker's questions are concrete.

let's put it together

the Division of Youth Employment and Guidance Service of the United States Employment Service, defines the disadvantaged as "those who have heavy liabilities which lessen their chances for competing successfully with their fellow citizens in all phases of life."

6 Welfare may help feed these unfortunate children; housing programs may improve their shelter; but the only thing that will really increase their chances of ever competing successfully with their fellow citizens in all phases of life is education. We must provide them with the kind of educational experiences that will make them interested in learning and will accelerate their academic achievement. To this end, Project Head Start was created. It is my purpose today to inform you of this project, to identify first the special problems of the disadvantaged child that must be overcome and then to relate how Head Start seeks to ameliorate them.

Paragraph 6 is the speaker's transition to the body of his speech. It begins by heightening the significance of his subject through eliminating alternative factors as suitable solutions to the problem. He does this through simple assertion, expecting the listener to agree. Every speaker must make assumptions about his auditors. He cannot possibly prove every statement he makes. It is vital therefore that he speak from the right premises or that he make proper assumptions. If he makes wrong assumptions, and asserts what needs to be proved, for example, he is likely to fail in his basic objective, be it to inform or to persuade his listeners.

In this case, the speaker states that education is the answer to the problem of the disadvantaged child and then identifies his specific solution, "Head Start." To make listening easier, he proceeds to lay out the basic compartments of his address. This type of forecasting of main points is often used as a clarity device and, if done well, usually is effective.

7 Most people agree that one of the primary problems confronting the disadvantaged child when he enters school is a marked lack of language skills. In the middle-class home environment, the preschool child is exposed to experiences that build his vocabulary and develop his ability to express himself. Think back to your early childhood. You were probably raised on *Mother Goose, Goldilocks and the Three Bears,* and other childhood fantasies. Your parents read these epic tales to you. While they were reading to you, you began to associate words and their meanings, and you also learned how to discriminate between word sounds. Slowly your basic vocabulary increased. Your parents talked to you, answered your questions, satisfied but yet increased your curiosity. Probably before you entered school, you could verbally recite the alphabet; possibly you were able to print the letters. And how about nursery school? Most of you probably went to nursery school and engaged in further language developing activities. When you started school, you were prepared to learn as you had mastered a basic vocabulary.

8 In contrast, let us talk about Willie, a Negro boy of six living in a slum area of a Midwestern metropolitan area. Willie's block is typical of any other in the area—a dimly lit, narrow street covered

The speaker now moves directly to the first problem area of the disadvantaged child. His plan of development is to contrast the preschool background of the average middle-class child with that of a slum child and then to clinch the point by citing two experimental studies. He does a good job of "up and down" speaking at this point. His initial statement of the point is of course at the abstract level, but it immediately moves to the personal and the concrete.

He uses Willie, a boy living in a slum area, as a contrast to the middle-class child. Willie represents all slum children. The speaker thus uses a story to describe the plight of the slum child, but not so for the middle-class child. Rather than let one person in a story represent all middle-class children, he lets each member of his audience be the main character in unfolding that drama. He asks each one to reflect back to his preschool days and recall experiences that develop language and speech skills. This technique gains audience involvement and makes the idea personal to everyone.

let's put it together

by the heavy shade of elms. Rusting cars are parked along the curb, children can be seen playing in the street, stopping only for a passing car. Willie's home is an old one-story, frame house built around 1900. Its brown, weather-beaten boards yearn to tell of days when it was in a white neighborhood. The home is in a state of disrepair—the screens are rusting and have holes in them, a front step is broken, a corner of the porch is falling.

9 Willie is the youngest of five children, the oldest being thirteen. His mother works nights at a hospital as a scrubwoman, earning sixty dollars a week; his father deserted the family when Willie was five months old. Willie's mother never completed the eighth grade. It is doubtful if his brothers or sisters will either. Until he started kindergarten, a year ago, Willie never saw a book, much less handled or looked through one. He never knew what a common item such as a crayon was. Ordinary childhood games were strange to him. He never conversed with any adult except his mother, but that was rare. When Willie started kindergarten last fall, he was frightened by the new experience. He spurned any attempts of the teacher to befriend him. He avoided any of the other children and would not join in their games. Willie had little or no applicable vocabulary, and he was not able to converse with anyone. He was unable to listen to anyone tell him anything for he was not yet able to associate word sounds with their meanings. He was very restless—a restlessness caused by acute hunger. He had no individuality of his own, just a black face in the crowd.

10 Now let me tell you of a recent experiment. A group of mothers from low-income neighborhoods were paid to read aloud for fifteen to twenty minutes a day to their infants less than a year old and before they learned to speak. The results: When these children were one and a half they showed significantly better language development than a like group of children who had not had the benefit of this experience.

11 Let me tell you of another experiment that seems to prove that if children do not have names for things, they don't really see them. The researcher took a group of children and gave each of them a butterfly. He then showed them a collection of butterflies and asked them to find one that matched the one they already had. Initially, the children could match the butterflies only by color, paying no attention to the patterns and designs on their wings. The researcher then divided the children into two groups. One of the groups he gave words for the patterns—such as "spots" or "stripes." Even the

The experiments document the speaker's point about language development; they provide quantification. They also provide an element of interest. The speaker recounts how the experiments were conducted, thus giving them story elements. They involve people and the findings involve suspense. People are intrinsically interested in how things come out.

youngest member of this group now could match the butterflies accurately and quickly. This was not true, however, of the children who had not been given verbal labels for the patterns on the butterflies' wings.

12 Can you see from these experiments what disadvantages Willie had when he started in school?

Ernie Link concludes his account of the experiments by relating them to Willie. He does this by asking the audience if they now can see his disadvantages. This question effectively identifies Willie, a specific slum child, to the general conclusions of the experiments.

13 Language skills are basic to learning when the child enters school. The child from the disadvantaged home simply does not have the kinds of experiences at home that produce great language development. The handicap with which he enters school is severe.

Paragraph 13 summarizes the first point about language development with a statement that reiterates the essence of it. The speaker here moves back up to the abstract level. This point could be strengthened considerably by testimony—a very short quotation from a recognized authority would verify the speaker's own conclusions.

14 A second critical handicap of the disadvantaged child when he enters school is a basic lack of curiosity. He often has little or no motivation for learning. Children are by nature curious; they have an innate desire to know. The normal, healthy preschool child asks the questions, "Why?" and "How come?" many times daily, often to the complete distraction of his parents. But the helpful parent

The basic plan of Ernie Link's second point is similar to that of his first. He initiates his discussion by stating the second handicap of disadvantaged children. Link then contrasts the slum child's background with that of the middle-class child, once more using an example to illuminate the slum child's plight. His development of the middle-class child's background, however, will respect these questions and attempt to answer them; never will he tell the child to shut up and stop asking so many silly questions. The child's curiosity is stimulated and he, in turn, finds learning exciting. To him the world is indeed a great, big, wonderful place to live in. His background is broadened by trips to the zoo, by parents reading stories to him, and by a train ride to a neighboring city. His storehouse of information is expanded. His parents value education and the child comes to school with a burning desire to know. He wants to read, to write, and to tell time. He wants to learn about caterpillars and butterflies.

lacks interest value compared to his approach in the first point when he directly involved the audience. In this instance, he refers to the middle-class child's experiences in the abstract. Consider the added interest value this same paragraph has when written differently.

This paragraph tells a story with a main character who has a name. It does not deal with the middle-class child in the abstract, it deals with Billy, the speaker's nephew. The paragraph is thus concrete; has interest value; and once again relates the speaker to his subject.

A second critical handicap of the disadvantaged child when he enters school is a basic lack of curiosity. He often has little or no motivation for learning. Children are by nature curious; they have an innate desire to know. The normal healthy preschool child asks the questions, "Why?" and "How come?" many times daily, often to the complete distraction of his parents. My nephew Billy is such a child. My sister, Billy's mother, tells me that he must ask the question at least fifty times a day. Although tormenting as his questions often are to them, his parents respect them and answer them; never do they tell him to shut up and go to

his room for asking too many questions. Billy finds learning exciting. The world is filled with adventure and is indeed a great, big, wonderful place to live in. On his second birthday, as a special present, his parents took him to the zoo. They went by train, since Billy was very interested in trains at that time. He has been to the zoo many times since. Every night at bedtime his parents read stories to him. Billy realizes that his parents value education and he will enter school with a burning desire to know. He wants to read, to write, and to tell time. He wants to learn about caterpillars and butterflies.

let's put it together

145

15 But what is the plight of the disadvantaged child? In a New York City school, a kindergarten teacher asked, "What animals eat carrots?" and one little girl quickly replied, "Rats." Her world was one of an alcoholic mother, ten brothers and sisters, an unknown father, a hungry stomach, filth—and rats. When she began asking questions of her mother, she got an abrupt "yes" or "no" or was punished for asking too many questions. She quickly learned not to ask.

16 Such children frequently have little knowledge of cultural items, little understanding of their home environment, and none of the world beyond a range of three to four blocks. They usually have few intellectual concepts and almost no ability to associate with other people. Some of these children do not know the names of colors or the simplest household objects. Many have never seen a book or held a pencil or used scissors to cut paper. A careful study of a group of disadvantaged children in fourth grade at one inner-city school showed that their average achievement level was one full year below their grade placement—a typical situation in any slum area.

The incident of the New York City child in paragraph 15 is pathetically funny. It tends to receive a small chuckle but, at the same time, makes a vivid impression upon the listener. The speaker effectively uses this story as a point of departure for elaborating the basic lack of curiosity-arousing experiences these children have.

He once more refers to an empirical study. The data of the study are pertinent and meaningful, but they lose a degree of believability because the source is not given. It would have been very easy for the speaker to be specific as to source rather than vaguely say, "A careful study of a group of disadvantaged children in fourth grade at one inner-city school . . ."

17 The Swiss psychologist Piaget uses the term "schema" for intellectual operations. He says that a schema arises as an adaptive measure but only as a consequence of the organism's interactions with the environment. In other words, experience is necessary to the development of intelligence. Piaget says that the more new things a child has seen and heard, the more he wants to see and hear. It arouses his curiosity. Psychologists today feel that what a child sees, hears, and learns before the age of four largely determines his basic intelligence at maturity. After a child is four, his I.Q. potential is more or less fixed, but before that his ability to improve is astounding. If this is true, how can the slum child with his three-block world be expected to compete with the child who has experienced travel, books, and educational toys? How can the child whose natural curiosity has been squashed by an unsympathetic adult keep up with the one whose questions were answered and who was given a feeling of self-importance?

18 Curiosity and a desire to learn are necessary to academic achievement. School for the disadvantaged child, who often possesses neither, is a frustrating experience.

In paragraph 17, the speaker concludes his second point with an appeal to authority. He first refers to Piaget and then to psychologists in general. He probably is safe in assuming that his listening audience has at least heard of Piaget and he need not qualify him beyond referring to him as "the Swiss psychologist." He also assumes that his audience will accept the general use of the term "psychologists" instead of referring to any specific group or using names. Do you think that he is safe in making this assumption? Ernie Link's references to leading psychologists doubtlessly strengthens his second point and increases its believability.

Simple elaboration, contrast, empirical data, and testimony are the tools the speaker uses in developing his second point. Interest level remains reasonably high.

Paragraph 18 again is a concluding restatement of the point the speaker has just completed. These restatements have the effect of rounding off the point and of assuring message clarity. They also create a definite and meaningful division between the main points of the speech.

let's put it together

19 A third barrier to academic achievement that disadvantaged children often encounter is a basic difficulty with authority. Doing what the teacher expects and what class discipline requires is incomprehensible to them at first. They often act impulsively and appear callous in the face of another's hurt or trouble. The authority they have experienced has been one of physical force. They have suffered and they are used to seeing people suffer. The concept of cooperation or concerted action is unknown to them. One has to grab that which he can get in order to survive, even if it means inflicting pain upon someone else. Love is foreign to them. Hate envelops them. These children need to develop a basic respect for self-discipline and for imposed discipline before they can enter into the spirit of the classroom. They must gain control of inner destructive impulses, turn aggression into hard work, and hitting to talking.

20 Physical problems are a fourth critical handicap that must be eliminated or diminished before disadvantaged children will improve academically. My baby sister entered kindergarten this fall. What is outstanding about her other than that she is my sister and everybody in my family thinks she is the cutest kid alive? She has exceptionally good health. From earliest infancy she

The speaker finds it important to include this third point about discipline but seems to lack material on the subject. The point is only briefly developed and lacks the careful design of the first two points. There is no contrast, no example, no testimony, no quantification, and no rhetorical question. A specific example or two would make the point much more vivid. The illustrative material of the previous points may, however, have some carry-over value concerning the believability of this point. The point also has a definite emotional tone that gives it a certain attention value—love, hate, and physical force. How do you as a reader feel about this point?

For his fourth point, the speaker returns to the design of his first two: contrast, illustration, and quantification. This time, however, he reverses himself and uses an example of the middle-class child. Previously he has spoken of middle-class children as a group and disadvantaged children individually. At the risk of being maudlin, he uses his baby sister as an example, has had the care of a pediatrician. She has had regular checkups, as prescribed by the doctor. Once when she had a minor physical ailment, it was corrected immediately. She never has had any problems with her teeth. Of course, she has been brushing them regularly since her second birthday. I will never forget how proud she was of her new, blue toothbrush when she got it as one of her presents. In the final analysis, Janet, my little sister, is a bundle of energy. She is perpetual motion. So much so that my mother says she is impossible to keep up with. Mrs. Johnson, my baby sister's teacher, says that Janet is doing very well in school. She is a healthy, happy child who wants to learn everything she can. My little sister Janet is not too different from the average middle-class child entering school. Most have had the same advantages Janet has had. You can probably verify this by thinking of the children you know.

21 On the other hand, Irwin Ross reports in an article in the *Reader's Digest* that in a study of 1,150 disadvantaged children entering school, 100 had visual problems, 12 had tuberculosis, 10 had serious hearing defects, and 575—more than half—had nutritional defects. Another group of testings showed that 441 out of 1,221 were

telling of her good health and physical energy. The story points up the kind of medical and dental care the average middle-class child gets today. He ends the paragraph (20) by generalizing from his little sister to the average middle-class child entering school, asking the listener to verify this statement himself by thinking of the children he knows. It, of course, is not difficult for most of us to think of some healthy, bouncing children living in our block; perhaps we even have close relatives who come to mind.

It may be questioned if it was even necessary for the speaker to illustrate the good health of the middle-class child. One might assume that the listening audience was already fully aware of this and the speaker could have gone directly from his statement of his fourth point to the health problems of the disadvantaged. How vital do you think the story of Janet is? Would the speech decline significantly in interest at this point if it were removed?

Paragraph 21 presents the contrast of the handicapped child. The speaker draws from an article by Irwin Ross in the *Reader's Digest* that illuminates the critical nature of the health problem of the disadvantaged child when he enters school. The statistics cited give impact to the point. Although some might wish that emotionally disturbed, 67 of them seriously. In some instances "slow learning" was a dental problem, and "discipline" problems turned out to be medical problems. Such children as those in this study often are listless in school and do poorly simply because they lack physical energy. Many of them enter kindergarten without having learned to wash their hands before eating. Even fewer have seen a toothbrush—to say nothing of using one regularly.

the speaker had *gone beyond the Reader's Digest* for his evidence, few listeners would doubt the veracity of the claim that disadvantaged children have terrific health handicaps.

22 Such are the problems of the disadvantaged child when he enters school. These four things —*language, curiosity, discipline,* and *physical health*—are the basic factors that must be improved before the child will be successful in school. It can make him a good student or a poor student. These are the factors that Head Start tries to deal with. It tries to prepare the disadvantaged child to compete with his middle-class neighbor when he starts in school.

Paragraph 22 serves as a summary statement of the problem phase of the speech and as a transition to the second major portion of the address. Such definite signposting is of great help to the average listener. By repeating what has gone before so that the auditor may the better recall it and by indicating where the speech is going next, it becomes one of the most effective clarity devices available to the speaker.

23 Project Head Start was created in February of 1965 when a committee of child care experts headed by Dr. Robert E. Cook, Chairman of the Department of Pediatrics at Johns Hopkins Medical School, suggested to the Office of Economic Opportunity that preschool development centers be established around the country. Dr. Cook in his recommendation states, "A program of this type

Paragraph 23 gives information concerning the inception of the Head Start Program. As such, it introduces a broader discussion of how the program seeks to cope with the four problems outlined earlier. The paragraph could well have been introduced earlier in the speech, perhaps at the first mention of Head Start. If dramatized and made more interesting, it might even must be comprehensive, involving activities generally associated with the fields of health, social services, and education." To fulfill this requirement, 45,000 teachers, doctors, nurses, and social workers were employed. They were supplemented by thousands of paid and unpaid volunteers. Head Start was initiated in the summer of 1965 with an enrollment of 560,000 youngsters in 2,400 communities. It has as its objective the preparation of disadvantaged youngsters for regular school activities. The program is geared toward overcoming the four critical problem areas I have identified.

24   Various plans and methods have been developed so these goals may be achieved. When the child has been selected for Head Start, a physical and psychological examination is given. The child is also given immunizations; dental care; eye, speech, and hearing examinations; and if treatment is necessary it is provided. Head Start seeks to promote the child's over-all health, physical growth, and motor development. The children are taught to wash their hands before eating, to eat a well-balanced meal in the cafeteria, and to use a knife, fork, and spoon. For a majority of children, the meal they receive in the cafeteria is likely to be the only substantial meal they get. For many of these youngsters a good nutri-

have been an effective introduction to this speech. Although low in interest value, the paragraph provides useful and meaningful insight into Operation Head Start that helps one to understand the remainder of the speech.

The speaker puts first things first in relating how Head Start operates. Head Start begins by taking a look at the physical well-being of the child before it tries to improve his mental capacities. This makes good sense. On the other hand, in developing the four problems in the first portion of his speech, Ernie Link found it convenient to deal with language and speech first, then with curiosity, discipline, and physical problems. Does this inverse approach to the second portion of the speech bother you? Usually good speech design dictates that the speaker use the same order in unfolding his solution as he used in developing his problem.

let's put it together

tional meal has amazing results: the tired become energetic, the slow begin to learn, and the undisciplined start to conform.

25 Verbal development and listening skills are stressed in Head Start. To build vocabulary, a picture book may be used during story time with the children participating in telling the story. Another technique employed to build vocabulary is that the teacher will show an object to the class and ask, "What is this?" The students are to respond with the name of the object. The teacher might ask, "Do you want to color?" The intended answer is, "Yes, I want to color." The teacher also tries to get these children to talk to each other. She may have them talk to each other over toy phones; have them use hand puppets; or have them play word games when the child has progressed enough that the teacher feels he should be able to talk to a group of children. The simplest kinds of show-and-tell situations are also utilized. Sometimes she may have the children find a picture in a book or magazine and tell about it.

26 When a boy named Bruce first entered Head Start he could only communicate with others by pushing or hitting. A few weeks later his face lit up whenever his teachers spoke to him. Bruce realized that his teachers would listen

Paragraphs 25 and 26 elaborate about how Head Start copes with the language problem. This point has two basic parts: first, a short explanation of teaching techniques; and second, two examples of children who have been helped by Head Start. The speaker can obviously not give a detailed explanation of teaching procedure for developing communication skills; he thus hopes to present enough examples of teaching techniques so as to give the listener a general idea of the approaches used. The illustration of Billy and the Kickapoo girl serve as visualization of the results of Head Start teaching. The speaker, however, fails to cite any empirical data of how much language development occurs in children from the Head Start experience. This is, of course, a deviation from the plan he followed earlier when he relied heavily upon research studies. Do you think that his audience would find the point believable as it is? Or do you feel that research evidence is vital for this point? The critical factors, of course, would be how much his listeners know about Head Start and how skeptical they are of it.

patiently to him while he stammered out the words he wanted to say. He learned to keep his hands to himself and to play less roughly as his verbal skills increased. A five-year-old Kickapoo Indian girl entered her Head Start class unable to speak a word of English. Two weeks later, swinging around on a carrousel she sang out, "By-by teacher." She picked up enough English in her Head Start class to get into the first grade the next year.

27 Head Start tries to arouse the children's curiosity by giving them badly needed contact with the outside world. Numerous field trips are set up. These field trips provide a chance to build vocabulary as they expand the children's experiences. Many of these children have never been downtown or ridden on a bus. In fact, it has been reported that some do not even know what a bus is. Many of them have never seen a skyscraper or traffic signals. Few have ridden on an elevator; hardly any in a taxicab. A large number have never seen animals other than cats, dogs, and rats. The zoo always provides excellent stimuli for these children. Sometimes they open up with spontaneous remarks as they see the zoo animals. Some even begin to ask questions.

28 Head Start provides $130 per thirty children for bus trips.

Paragraphs 27 and 28 consist of the solution phase to the curiosity problem. The speaker again, in a selective manner, tells of Head Start procedures designed to attack the problem. He cites how much money the Head Start program provides for bus trips and then presents two examples of instances where local people pitched in and provided special assistance, ending on the sentimental but meaningful note of one store giving each child a toy to take home, a gesture that perhaps more than any other would let the child know that there are people who care.

The development of this point seems too narrow in .focus. Although field trips are vital to the arousal of curiosity in the disadvantaged child, one gets the impression that this is the only approach used. Curiosity-arousing programs occur in the schoolroom as

However, one Head Start class in Charlotte, North Carolina, raised $45 for a bus trip by putting on a talent show. The City Council of Charlotte raised $90 to entertain and provide lunch for the youngsters. Local businesses donated ice drinks and socks to the children. But best of all, one of the department stores gave each child a toy to take home and keep.

29 As the child's physical well-being improves, his behavior improves; as his intellectual curiosity is stimulated, his mind is occupied more and more with learning; as his language develops, his need to communicate by hitting and kicking lessens. The Head Start teacher strives to help the child gain control of inner destructive impulses, to turn aggression into hard work, hitting to talking; she attempts to increase the child's understanding of the difference between feeling angry and acting angry and to develop sympathy for the difficulties of others. The child often begins to find his relationships with authority figures quite satisfying. No longer does the authority figure merely tell him to shut up or cuff him in the mouth. Rather he shows interest in the child and

well, and the speaker would have done well to mention this. Again, there are no data in the development of this point that show that curiosity is actually improved by the Head Start experience.

Moreover, the speaker may be too general in developing this idea. Interest and meaning would be intensified if he took a typical Head Start school and told of its program as illustration of the point. He could thereby inject exact names and places into the development, as well as tell it in story form.

The speaker begins this section with a nice parallelism telling what effect communication skills and curiosity have upon the child's behavior. From time to time, Ernie Link uses parallel phrasing and parallel sentence structure to achieve a rhythmical effect (see, for example, paragraph 31). This stylistic device is easy to employ and gives added polish and impact to the address.

The entire point is developed by assertion. No examples, no quantification. Apparently the speaker assumes that this will be common sense to his audience. What do you think? A general criticism of this speech may well be that the speaker documents his "problem" points well but fails in this respect with his "solution" points. This encourages him to express his thoughts and his feelings. Self-esteem and real self-importance work against impulses to attract attention through physical means.

30 The first three years of the elementary school experience are critical to the child. If learning is not successful and satisfying in these years, the entire educational career of the child is jeopardized. This is why Head Start is so important. This is why Head Start warrants our support. This is why Head Start should be continued and should be expanded.

31 To be sure much more is needed. We need special follow-up to Head Start in kindergarten and in the early grades. We need special programs in our elementary schools for the disadvantaged. We need specially trained teachers to deal with these children. But at the same time if we can help our nation's underprivileged children to enter kindergarten with a better chance of success we will have

is a common speech failing. And unfortunately so, for very often people are much more ready to accept the statement of the problem than they are the workability of the proposed solution. This is probably true of this speech. People are more likely to accept the contention that disadvantaged children are handicapped in school than they are the claim that Head Start alleviates the problem. Examples and quantification of the positive effects of Head Start would very likely increase the believability of the speech for most people.

Paragraph 30 inaugurates the speaker's conclusion. It wisely restates the critical nature of the speech subject and relates it to Head Start. Note that the speaker scatters a summary throughout the conclusion. When one couples this paragraph with the statement of how Head Start would have helped Tommy and the quotation by Mrs. Johnson, one has all the vital aspects of the speech. Frequently, a speaker will summarize his address in one compact statement. This is good technique also. Regardless of the approach to the summary, the conclusion of most truly effective speeches will usually perform three basic functions: (1) focus sharply upon the basic message of the speech; (2) summarize, in some form, the basic content of the speech;

provided the basis for later programs. And if we really want to solve our delinquency problems, our unemployment problems, or our ghetto problems, we have the best chance of doing this by starting the child off in the right direction when he first enters school.

32 In my mind's eye I can still see Tommy's red toy tractor with one wheel missing lying on a patch of dry, brown crabgrass. I can still see Tommy looking down silently at the top of his small wooden desk when asked a question by his teacher. I can still see the agony Tommy suffered from being unable to compete with the other children in his class. Head Start would have been invaluable to him. It would have helped his language development; it would have improved his ability to speak; it would have given him many of the kinds of experiences that most of the other children had had at home and at nursery school.

33 Initially describing Project Head Start, Mrs. Lyndon B. Johnson called it an effort to reach out to the younger children "lost in a grey world of poverty and neglect." She said, "Some don't know even a hundred words. Some don't know how to sit in a chair because they don't have as much

(3) round off the speech effectively, lifting it to a meaningful and climactic ending. The conclusion should doubtlessly produce a final impact. Ernie Link's conclusion performs these functions admirably.

Paragraph 32 returns the listener to the setting with which the speech was begun. Tommy is again brought to mind. This technique produces at least three salutary effects: (1) it gives the speech a desired cohesiveness; (2) it concretely illustrates the good that would come from Head Start for our nation's Tommies; and (3) it once more relates the speech to the speaker. On the other hand, this is a highly emotional paragraph and may strike some listeners as too maudlin. Manner of presentation might thus be vital for believability. What is your assessment? How do you think the average college class would react to this paragraph? Do you think most other audiences would react differently?

The closing quotation is used to give one final mention of the intensity of the problem, thereby offering at least a partial summary, and to end the speech on a high note. Since this speech really is about extending a helping hand to the disadvantaged child, "Come take my hand" is a most apas a chair. Some have never seen a book or held a flower. . . . There is no more important task in our communities, than for such children to hear a voice say, 'Come take my hand.' "

propriate ending note. Packed with emotion and imagery, it meaningfully punctuates the entire address.

epilogue

A schoolboy, asked by his teacher to review a book on the care and feeding of penguins, began his report with the lament: "This book tells me more about penguins than I'm interested in knowing." In contrast to our report-writing schoolboy, we hope that this book has told you less about speechmaking than you would like to know. Much more could be said. Quintilian, for example, wrote a twelve-volume treatise on the subject and called it *The Institutes of Oratory*. Our goal has not been to say everything there is to say, but to cover those basic principles especially useful to the beginning speaker. We have tried to follow our own advice—to be relevant, clear, interesting, and believable—so that you may do not only as we say, but also as we do.

Let us end with Aristotle's advice to the speaker who is closing his presentation: "I have done; you all have heard; you have the facts; give your judgment."

index

index

162